VANT TO
OF THESE
:IPES!

TABLE OF CONTENTS

A BRIEF HISTORY OF THE KETOGENIC DIET

The ketogenic diet has gotten popular recently as an effective fat loss diet. But it was originally designed in the 1920s by Dr. Russell Wilder at the Mayo Clinic.

Dr. Wilder used ketogenic diets as an effective treatment for epilepsy in children. However, after anti-seizure medications became widely available, the ketogenic diet fell out of favor.

From 1940 until almost 1980, there was little interest in ketogenic diets.

Then, the popularity of low-carb (or Atkins) diets started to rekindle interest. And the rise of Paleo diets has prompted a full resurgence of interest in the ketogenic diet.

This time, though, the primary focus is weight loss and health.

In 2013, the ketogenic diet was the 5th most-searched-for diet on Google. Since that time, its popularity has only increased.

In fact, a clinical trial began in 2015 to test the impact of a keto diet on type 2 diabetes and pre-diabetes. The results aren't out yet, of course. Still, more research is now underway to understand the benefits of keto diets.

WHAT IS A KETOGENIC DIET?

A keto or ketogenic diet is a diet plan that helps your body achieve nutritional ketosis.

That means your body is relying primarily on fat and ketones (rather than sugar) for its energy. Ketones are produced when your body breaks down fat.

The cells in your body can create energy from one of four sources. They can use fat, carbohydrate, protein, or ketones.

When you go on a ketogenic diet, you force the cells in your body to primarily use fat and ketones for fuel. And there are several benefits of doing this, which I'll explain in a bit.

Most people can achieve nutritional ketosis by eating a lot of fat, moderate amounts of protein, and few carbohydrates.

But there are also many mistakes I see people make. So please make sure to read the section on page 7 titled " MISTAKES TO AVOID ON A KETOGENIC DIET."

First...

Ditch the sugar and eat real foods!

IS A KETOGENIC DIET SAFE?

First, a quick disclaimer. I am not a doctor, medical professional, or nutritionist. Any suggestions provided in this book are not a substitute for medical or nutritional advice. You should definitely consult your physician before beginning any exercise or nutrition program.

With all that in mind, the answer is generally yes. A ketogenic diet is safe for healthy adults. But there is a lot of misinformation about keto diets. Consequently, many people will tell you that ketogenic diets are dangerous.

Here are a few quick facts you should know about the ketogenic diet and its safety:

1. Ketosis is NOT the Same as Ketoacidosis.

Many people (including medical professionals) get confused about this. Ketosis is when your body uses ketones as its primary energy source (instead of glucose).

Ketoacidosis is something altogether different. First of all, it's a serious medical condition. It usually occurs in a few different situations:

- Type 1 diabetes.
- Alcoholic binges.
- End-stage Type 2 diabetes.
- Extended periods of starvation (over the course of months).
- Prolonged severe exercise.
- A few cases of Ecstasy use have caused ketoacidosis.

In ketoacidosis, the body produces an excessive amount of ketones. That causes the blood to become acidic, which can be quite dangerous.

In a healthy adult, the body will regulate the amount of ketones produced so that this doesn't happen. For instance, the body will release insulin to stop the burning of fats.

Eating a ketogenic diet or even fasting for a few days will NOT cause an overload of ketones.

2. Carbohydrates are NOT Essential

This is another common misconception.

Protein, some fats, and many vitamins and minerals are essential for the human body. Carbohydrates, however, are not essential.

Cells that lack a mitochondrion (such as some very small neurons and red blood cells) always need a small amount of glucose. But even in ketosis, your body can easily fill those needs by turning protein into glucose.

This is how you can live for 40-60 days without eating. Your body converts fat stores into ketones, which your body then uses for energy.

3. Pay Attention To Your Gut Health

Over the years, this is one of the biggest mistakes I've seen people make.

Meat and seafood are great, but your gut won't thrive on those foods alone. You must make sure to eat plenty of vegetables that are high in fiber to support your gut.

The bacteria and other microorganisms in your gut need prebiotic fiber and resistant starch to do their job.

So besides fibrous veggies, also consume probiotics, prebiotics (check out CoBionic Foundation for this!), and fermented foods on a regular basis.

I highly recommend a green smoothie to start the day (check out the recipe on page 13).

KETO VS LOW CARB VS PALEO

In most ways, a ketogenic diet is very similar to a low carb diet. In particular, you must restrict carbohydrates in both diets.

The difference is that a ketogenic diet is all about making sure that your body is in ketosis. While eating low-carb is a big part of that, it's not the only thing you should think about.

Some people can eat a high amount of daily carbs and still be in nutritional ketosis. Other people need to eat much fewer carbs and also make other adjustments to achieve the same state. Men usually seem to have it easier than women in this respect.

I like to think of a ketogenic diet as a more precise version of a low-carb diet. You're paying closer attention to what's going on in your body. Rather than focusing only on how many carbs you eat, you're ensuring that your body is burning fat for energy.

I'm also a huge proponent of the Paleo diet, and the way I suggest everyone does Keto is with a Paleo Keto diet. That means eating real foods that nourish your body instead of just counting macros.

But please don't get stuck on the labels. In the end, you can be on a low-carb, ketogenic, or even Paleo diet, and still be eating exactly the same foods!

Each diet places a slight emphasis on a different aspect of what you eat, but the results can be identical.

Most people would consider every recipe in this cookbook to be Keto, Low Carb, and Paleo (as well as dairy-free, sugar-free, grain-free, and gluten-free!).

My best suggestion is to forget about the classifications. Instead, ask yourself these questions about the food you eat:

What is this food doing for or to my body?

Does this food provide me with nutrients (e.g., vitamins, minerals, essential amino acids, etc.)?

Does this food contain toxins (gluten, processed sugar, etc.) that could prevent my body from functioning well?

Does this food hinder my body from staying in ketosis?

WILL A KETOGENIC DIET HELP ME LOSE WEIGHT?

A ketogenic diet is not magic. Without a doubt, some people have more success than others. So I can't guarantee any particular results.

However, I have seen many people lose a lot of weight with ketogenic diets. And I truly believe that a ketogenic diet is one of the most effective and healthiest ways to lose weight.

There are a few big reasons why ketogenic diets work so well...

1. Controlling Hunger

This is the single biggest reason that ketogenic diets are great. And it's also the biggest reason that most other diets fail.

Ketogenic diets help your body's regulation of hormones and neurotransmitters. One of the results is that you get much less hungry.

That means reduced cravings for junk food, less cheating, and more weight loss.

If you've ever dieted before, then you know that sticking to it is the hardest part. Sticking to a ketogenic diet is much easier, because you don't face the same hunger.

2. Metabolic Flexibility

If you've been eating a high-carb diet, then your body is excellent at burning carbohydrates for energy.

That makes sense when you're eating a lot of carbs. But it also means that your body is often not good at burning fat.

Ideally, your body should be able to switch back and forth between burning carbs and fat. When your body can't do this, it's called "poor metabolic flexibility."

In that case, you don't burn much fat, you get cravings for sugar and carbs, and you have a hard time losing weight. That's one of the reasons that you might get hungrier on a high-carb diet. If your body can't burn fat well, then you'll be hungry whenever your blood sugar is low.

A ketogenic diet can help you regain metabolic flexibility. By putting your body into a state of ketosis, you force your body to get better at burning fat.

And many people find that they end up burning a lot of their bodies' fat stores, which is exactly what you want for weight loss.

3. Hyper-Palatability

You might have never heard of hyper-palatable foods. Yet nothing has contributed to obesity more in modern times.

A food is hyper-palatable when it has a "magic" combination of fat, sugar, and salt. The result is that foods become addictive. You can't stop eating them, even if you're full.

And food manufacturers make use of that combination to create irresistible processed foods. From potato chips to cookies to donuts, humans have created a thousand addictive foods.

But none of these foods occur in nature. Fruits usually have sugar, and meats usually have fat, but you don't find foods with both.

By removing refined carbohydrates, a ketogenic diet also removes hyper-palatable foods. And that means you won't feel an unstoppable need to keep eating and eating.

The result is that most people feel less hungry and have fewer cravings.

This means you're effortlessly restricting your calorie intake, leading to more weight loss.

4. Inflammation and Toxins

Finally, a ketogenic diet also helps you to remove toxins and reduce inflammation.

You may not even see or be aware of chronic inflammation. But inflammation in your body is a big obstacle to weight loss.

And the main causes of inflammation are many of the foods you eat. The biggest culprits are wheat and other grains, milk, and processed sugar.

Coincidentally, these are all foods that you must avoid on a ketogenic diet.

MISTAKES TO AVOID ON A KETOGENIC DIET

In this section, I want to cover some of the mistakes that I often see people make on a ketogenic diet. If you can avoid these mistakes, then you'll be much more likely to lose weight and feel better.

Mistake #1: Bad Mindset

Many people treat the ketogenic diet as something they'll "try for a week or two."

They want to dip their toe in the water to see if the diet "works." But they definitely don't want to commit.

There are two problems with this approach. First of all, if you're not committed, then you're going to give up at the first sign of trouble. If you get tempted, or if you don't lose weight for a few days, then you'll give it all up. And I can guarantee that not everything will go perfectly for you. It never does.

The second problem is that no diet works unless you approach it as a lifestyle.

If you want, you can lose some weight and then go back to eating bread, pasta, and sugar. But if you go back to eating those foods, you'll also go back to gaining weight. That is what we call the yo-yo dieting trap.

Mistake #2: Eating Too Much

Many of us have developed bad eating habits. We'll eat until everything is gone on our plates, we'll eat when it's mealtime rather than when we're hungry. And we'll snack all day instead of eating real meals.

All of this unfortunately leads to a lot of overeating.

Mistake #3: Not Testing

Our bodies are all a little bit different. Two people eating the same ketogenic diet can sometimes get different results.

One person could be in ketosis and losing weight, and another person could be struggling.

That's why testing is so important. You need to make sure that you're actually in ketosis. And if you aren't, then you can make adjustments to your diet and life.

When you're in ketosis, your body will produce ketone bodies. There are 3 types of ketone bodies: Acetoacetate (AcAc), Beta-hydroxybutyrate (BHB), and Acetone.

In your blood, you can measure all 3 ketone bodies. In your urine, AcAc and Acetone can be measured. And in your breath, just Acetone.

Your blood ketone levels are the best indicator of ketosis. Unfortunately, measuring blood ketone levels is also the most expensive method.

That's why many people still measure their urine and breath ketone levels instead.

For weight loss, you don't need to chase high ketone levels - measuring and tracking ketones is just another way to get more data about what's happening in your body so don't get stuck on ketone levels!

the Essential
KETO

Mistake #4: Not Eating Enough Nutrient-Dense Foods

On a ketogenic diet, you'll pay a lot of attention to the macronutrients you eat and you can use our Keto Calculator to figure out the right proportion of fats, carbs, and protein for you: https://ketosummit.com/keto-calculator

But don't forget that you also need to be getting enough vitamins and minerals.

You might be aware of some terrible things that happen if you're severely deficient in a micronutrient. For example...

- You can get scurvy if you don't get enough vitamin C.
- You can get goiter if you're deficient in iodine.
- Or you could go blind if you don't get enough vitamin A.

> Another great test to consider is a DEXA scan. This test will measure your fat levels as well as your bone and muscle levels. If you do it before you start your diet, you'll be able to later track precisely how well your diet is working.

Besides those acute problems, chronic deficiencies can also be a huge problem. Often, nutrient deficiencies are not so severe that you exhibit a particular disease. That doesn't mean, though, that they're not making you less healthy.

Over time, if you're low in vitamins and minerals, your body just won't function well. That can lead to illnesses, fatigue, and more. Even minor vitamin and mineral deficiencies might be making it harder for you to lose weight.

An easy way to boost your micronutrient intake is to eat more nutrient-dense foods. Most of these foods fit well into a ketogenic diet.

For instance, green leafy vegetables, organ meats, and seafood are all ketogenic-friendly. And they're some of the most nutrient-dense foods you can eat.

Supplementation with a good multivitamin or greens powder is also helpful.

If you're into testing, then try getting a SpectraCell analysis or an Urine Organic Acid test. Both of these tests will tell you which vitamins and minerals you're deficient in. That way, you can focus specifically on those deficiencies.

Mistake #5: Eating Toxic, Inflammatory Foods - Even if They're Low Carb

Not everything that is low in carbs is good for you. Period.

For example, you can go to most grocery stores these days and find low-carb processed foods. You can get low-carb bread, low-carb cookies, and low-carb snacks.

You might be able to stay in ketosis while eating those low-carb foods, but they're still bad for your body. Many of them contain wheat, gluten, and other inflammatory ingredients.

And as I mentioned, inflammation always makes it harder for you to lose weight.

Here are ingredients that I suggest avoiding, even in low-carb foods:

- Wheat, Rye, and Barley. New technology has created a way to make these foods low-carb sometimes. But they still always contain gluten, which will inevitably cause inflammation in your body. Plus, they're not very nutrient-dense.
- Dairy. Yes - even cheese. In the abstract, dairy might be ok. The problem is that you don't live in an abstract world. Milk will pretty much always keep you out of ketosis. And the vast majority of people have some level of sensitivity to dairy products like cheese. (This is most likely true even if you aren't lactose-intolerant.) Plus, you're likely to overeat cheese and cream!
- Vegetable and Seed Oils. This includes Vegetable Oil, Canola Oil, Corn Oil, Sunflower Oil, and similar products. Your cooking oil also makes a huge difference to your weight loss. As Dr. Shanahan points out in her book, Deep Nutrition, the production of these oils produces trans-fats, which can block your enzymes for burning fat.
- Any food you have an intolerance to. Start paying more attention to your body. If you wake up one day and notice that you're congested or that your joints are stiff, ask yourself what you ate. You're likely sensitive to one of the foods you ate the day before.

Also, be careful with nuts. Many people have allergies or sensitivities to nuts. But more than that, nuts are easy to overeat. Again, a ketogenic diet is not magic, so eating 3,000 calories of nuts per day is going to make a difference.

Mistake #6: Ignoring Sleep, Exercise, and Stress

While eating a good diet is important for weight loss, it's not all that matters.

Many weight-loss studies have stressed the importance of sleep (7+ hours), exercise, and de-stressing. It's tough to get everything right all at once. Still, any small efforts you make in these areas will pay off in the end.

Mistake #7: Not Being Patient

It can take up to two or three weeks to become keto-adapted. So if you're going to give the ketogenic diet a try, then actually give it a try and be patient.

It's taken you a lifetime of eating poorly to get to where you're at. You can't expect to fix all that damage in just a few weeks.

Mistake #8: Not Eating Enough Fiber

Mainstream nutrition has gotten a lot of things wrong.

The importance of fiber is not one of them. The past few years of scientific research has shown just how important fiber is for your gut health.

In particular, soluble fiber and resistant starches from vegetables can improve your gut bacteria. Fermented foods like sauerkraut are also excellent in this regard.

And if you have trouble eating enough vegetables then **take a good prebiotic like the CoBionic Foundation**.

WHAT IF A KETOGENIC DIET DOESN'T HELP ME LOSE WEIGHT?

This is a fear that I hear all the time...

"What if I put in all this effort - give up all these foods - and it still doesn't work?"

I completely understand this fear. I used to ask myself the same thing.

But this is also the reason why I don't believe in "dieting." Dieting is a short-term project where your only goal is to lose weight.

I'm not saying that you shouldn't try to lose weight. I think it's often a worthwhile goal.

But if that's your only goal, then you'll be disappointed if you go even a few days without any results. And in the world of weight loss, you will definitely have times when you stall a little bit.

A more practical way of thinking is to focus on doing the right things, rather than just on the results. Make it your goal every day to feed your body foods that give it energy, vitamins, and minerals.

Appreciate every healthy food you eat, knowing that it will give you lasting health. In that way, you'll naturally lose weight, keep it off, and gain better health as a result.

That's why this cookbook isn't just about replacing the carbs in your diet with other junk.

This is not just another low-carb cookbook.

Instead, this cookbook will help you focus on the principles behind the ketogenic diet. (And, of course, provide you with delicious ketogenic foods as well.)

I want you to lose weight. But I also want you to enjoy nutrient-dense and delicious foods that are low in toxins.

That way, there's no downside to eating recipes from this cookbook. Even if you don't lose weight immediately, you're still feeding your body nourishing foods.

At this point you might be thinking, "yeah, but what do I do if I still don't lose weight?"

I've helped thousands of people - through our website, books, programs and otherwise. So I won't lie to you and say that it never happens. Sometimes, someone will have an abnormally hard time losing weight.

If you're doing everything right but aren't getting results, then something else is going on in your body that you are not aware of. That's when I recommend you do some extensive testing with someone like Christopher Kelly from Nourish Balance Thrive.

It could be something as simple as having a gut pathogen. Or it could be something more complex like hypothyroidism or autoimmune disorders.

The point is this.

Diet is perhaps the most important part of losing weight. But it's still only a part. If your body is using energy and resources on an underlying health condition, weight loss is much harder.

However, in 98% of cases, getting your diet and lifestyle in order is enough. So don't jump to the conclusion that you have other issues.

WHAT CAN I EAT ON A KETOGENIC DIET?

Eat plenty of fats, moderate amounts of protein, and very little carbohydrates.

Carbohydrate Intake:

For some people, staying under 100g per day of carbohydrates will be pretty low carb. But, for most people, that number needs to be under 50g. For people with insulin resistance, you might need to consume under 30g or 20g per day.

If you are a serious athlete, then your carbohydrate intake may need to be higher than even 100g per day.

Estimated nutritional information is provided for every recipe in this cookbook to help you plan your meals.

To make it easier for you to get an estimate as to how much you should be eating, try using our Keto Calculator here:

https://ketosummit.com/keto-calculator

Please note that this calculator is designed only as a guide to how much you should be eating.

WHAT'S DIFFERENT ABOUT THIS COOKBOOK?

This cookbook contains recipes that will help you get into nutritional ketosis.

But as I pointed out above, a variety of other factors will determine if you're actually in ketosis. So, no matter what you eat, you might need to do some tweaking.

Nonetheless, these recipes (which are grain-free, soy-free, dairy-free, peanut-free, and free of seed oils) will help you reach ketosis while also providing your body with nutrient-dense meals to satisfy your hunger and heal your body.

Quick Note about Tamari Sauce, Ghee, Sesame Oil, and Keto Sweeteners:
These are 4 ingredients that people often ask about. This book doesn't go into the science and ideas behind the keto diet, but you can read about why these ingredients are ok to use on a keto diet here (and if you're not familiar with those ingredients, then those articles also explain what they are):

Tamari Sauce and Sesame Oil article -
https://ketosummit.com/keto-stir-fry-sauce

Ghee article -
https://ketosummit.com/is-ghee-keto

Stevia article -
https://ketosummit.com/stevia-keto

Erythritol article -
https://ketosummit.com/are-sugar-alcohols-keto

For Keto sweeteners, we suggest using natural ones like stevia, monk fruit, and erythritol.

If for any reason you'd prefer not to use these ingredients, you can:

- use Coconut Aminos instead of Tamari Sauce

- use Coconut Oil instead of Ghee

- use Olive Oil instead of Sesame Oil

- omit Stevia/Erythritol from the recipe.

FOUR TIPS FOR MEAL PLANNING ON A KETOGENIC DIET

If you're looking for detailed Keto Meal Plans, then check out https://mealplan.club/keto-meal-plans

There's also a 14-day Keto meal plan at the back of this book along with a batch cooking meal plan.

But I know everybody's tastes and lifestyles are different, so if you want to do your own meal planning, then here are four tips to help make your life easier:

1. Keep it simple

It's easy to fall off a diet if preparing the meals gets too complicated. So, remember to keep it simple. I love cooking a large batch of meat in the slow cooker, such as the slow cooker chicken and bacon or the oxtail stew. Then, we eat it over the next few days - each time with some veggie side dishes.

Or, for more variation, we sauté the meat with whatever veggies we have on hand. Or, we throw it into some bone broth with some veggies and make a quick soup out of it.

2. Eat the same foods on multiple days

It's easy to use up all your mental energy trying to figure out what to eat. Another way to keep it simple is to eat the same foods on multiple days. Breakfast is an easy meal to do this with. During the weekdays, choose an easy and nutritious breakfast recipe to make every day. The coconut ghee coffee or the breakfast green smoothie are both excellent options to start your day with.

3. Plan what you'll eat if you get stuck at work or can't eat at home

Many diets fail because you had one bad day at work, you went out to a restaurant with friends, or you went on vacation. At those times, all your great intentions vanish into thin air.

So try to plan ahead for those situations. Which local restaurant can you go to and order a steak and salad if you get home too late or you're too tired to cook?

Or if you're going out with friends, do you know exactly what you can order at the restaurant? That way, you don't even have to look at the menu again and get tempted.

4. Carry some snacks round with you

I suggest snacks like nuts, coconut butter, cacao nibs, or 100% dark chocolate to keep with you. If you do get hungry, then you can eat some of your snack rather than be tempted by foods that will derail your ketogenic diet. Just note that nuts, coconut butter, cacao nibs, and dark chocolate all do contain small amounts of net carbohydrates, so try not to overeat them!

the Essential
KETO
COOKBOOK

Breakfast

CHAPTER I

BREAKFAST GREEN SMOOTHIE

Prep Time: 5 minutes | *Cook Time:* 0 minutes | *Total Time:* 5 minutes
Yield: 1 serving
Nutritional Data (estimates) - per serving:
Calories: 380   Fat: 30 g   Net Carbohydrates: 5 g   Protein: 12 g

ingredients

- 2 cups *(60 g)* spinach (or other leafy greens)
- 1/3 cup *(46 g)* raw almonds
- 2 Brazil nuts
- 1 cup *(240 ml)* coconut milk (unsweetened - from refrigerated cartons not cans)
- 1 scoop *(20 g)* greens powder (optional)
- 1 Tablespoon *(10 g)* psyllium seeds (or psyllium husks) or chia seeds

instructions

1. Place the spinach, almonds, Brazil nuts, and coconut milk into the blender first.
2. Blend until pureed.
3. Add in the rest of the ingredients (greens powder, psyllium seeds) and blend well.

Green smoothies can be a great source of soluble dietary fiber - it'll help keep your gut bacteria functioning well. To boost up your fiber intake even more, add a scoop of CoBionic Foundation (prebiotic fiber)

the Essential
KETO
COOKBOOK

BACON LEMON THYME MUFFINS

Prep Time: 10 minutes | *Cook Time:* 20 minutes | *Total Time:* 30 minutes
Yield: 12 servings
Nutritional Data (estimates) - per serving:
Calories: 300   Fat: 28 g   Net Carbohydrates: 4 g   Protein: 11 g

ingredients
- 3 cups *(360 g)* almond flour
- 1 cup *(100 g)* bacon bits
- 1/2 cup *(120 ml)* ghee (or coconut oil), melted
- 4 eggs, whisked
- 2 teaspoons *(2 g)* lemon thyme (or use another herb of your choice)
- 1 teaspoon *(4 g)* baking soda
- 1/2 teaspoon *(2 g)* salt (optional)

instructions
1. Preheat oven to 350 F *(175 C)*.
2. Melt the ghee in a mixing bowl.
3. Add in the rest of the ingredients except the bacon bits to the mixing bowl.
4. Mix everything together well.
5. Lastly, add in the bacon bits.
6. Line a muffin pan with muffin liners. Spoon the mixture into the muffin pan (to around 3/4 full).
7. Bake for 18-20 minutes until a toothpick comes out clean when you insert it into a muffin.

CREAMY BREAKFAST PORRIDGE

Prep Time: 2 minutes | **Cook Time:** 5 minutes | **Total Time:** 7 minutes
Yield: 2 servings
Nutritional Data (estimates) - per serving:
Calories: 430   Fat: 40 g   Net Carbohydrates: 6 g   Protein: 8 g

ingredients

- 1/2 cup *(60 g)* almonds, ground using a food processor or blender
- 3/4 cup *(180 ml)* coconut milk
- Erythritol or stevia to taste (optional)
- 1 teaspoon *(2 g)* cinnamon powder
- Dash of nutmeg
- Dash of cloves
- Dash of cardamom (optional)

instructions

1. Heat the coconut milk in a small saucepan on medium heat until it forms a liquid.
2. Add in the ground almonds and sweetener and stir to mix in.
3. Keep stirring for approximately 5 minutes (it'll start to thicken a bit more).
4. Add in the spices (have a taste to check whether you want more sweetener or spices) and serve hot.

LEMON FRIED AVOCADOS

Prep Time: 2 minutes | *Cook Time:* 5 minutes | *Total Time:* 7 minutes
Yield: 2 servings
Nutritional Data (estimates) - per serving:
Calories: 200   Fat: 20 g   Net Carbohydrates: 2 g   Protein: 2 g

ingredients
- 1 ripe avocado (not too soft), cut into slices
- 1 Tablespoon *(15 ml)* coconut oil
- 1 Tablespoon *(15 ml)* lemon juice
- Salt to taste (or lemon salt)

Make sure to keep an eye on these as they burn quickly!

instructions
1. Add coconut oil to a frying pan. Place the avocado slices into the oil gently.
2. Fry the avocado slices (turning gently) so that all sides are slightly browned.
3. Sprinkle the lemon juice and salt over the slices and serve warm.

EASY SEED & NUT GRANOLA

Prep Time: 5 minutes | *Cook Time:* 0 minutes | *Total Time:* 5 minutes
Yield: 1 serving
Nutritional Data (estimates) - per serving:
Calories: 400   Fat: 30 g   Net Carbohydrates: 9 g   Protein: 9 g

ingredients
- Small handful of nuts (10 almonds, 3 Brazil nuts, 5 cashews)
- 2 Tablespoons *(17 g)* pumpkin seeds
- 1 Tablespoon *(12 g)* cacao nibs
- 1 Tablespoon *(5 g)* coconut flakes
- 1/4 cup *(60 ml)* unsweetened coconut or almond milk

instructions
1. Mix together all the dry ingredients. If you're making a large batch, then store leftovers in an airtight container. Serve with coconut or almond milk.

ALMOND BUTTER CHOCO SHAKE

Prep Time: 5 minutes | **Cook Time:** 0 minutes | **Total Time:** 5 minutes
Yield: 1 serving
Nutritional Data (estimates) - per serving:
Calories: 190   Fat: 15 g   Net Carbohydrates: 7 g   Protein: 4 g

ingredients
- 1 cup *(240 ml)* coconut milk or almond milk
- 2 Tablespoons *(10 g)* unsweetened cacao powder
(or 1 scoop CoBionic Indulgence for added collagen)
- 1 Tablespoon *(16 g)* almond butter
- 1 teaspoon *(5 ml)* vanilla extract
- 1/4 cup *(35 g)* ice (optional)
- Erythritol or stevia to taste (optional)

instructions
1. Place all the ingredients into a blender and blend well.

EGG AND HAM ROLLS

Prep Time: 10 minutes | **Cook Time:** 15 minutes | **Total Time:** 25 minutes
Yield: 4 servings
Nutritional Data (estimates) - per serving:
Calories: 158   Fat: 12 g   Net Carbohydrates: 1 g   Protein: 12 g

ingredients
- 4 slices of ham
- 1 cucumber, sliced thin
- 4 eggs, whisked well
- 2 Tablespoons *(30 ml)* avocado oil, to cook with

instructions
1. Add 1 teaspoon of avocado oil to a frying pan on low to medium heat and spread it around with a paper towel.
2. Add 1/4 cup of whisked eggs to the pan and roll it around to spread it thin.
3. Place a lid on top of the frying pan and let it cook until the base of the egg wrap is cooked (approx. 2-3 minutes). Carefully place on a plate and let cool.
4. Repeat in batches with the rest of the egg mixture to make egg wraps.
5. Create rolls with the egg wraps, slices of ham, and cucumber slices.

KALE AND CHIVES EGG MUFFINS

Prep Time: 10 minutes | *Cook Time:* 30 minutes | *Total Time:* 40 minutes
Yield: 4 servings
Nutritional Data (estimates) - per serving:
Calories: 240   Fat: 20 g   Net Carbohydrates: 3 g   Protein: 12 g

ingredients

- 6 eggs
- 1 cup kale, finely chopped
- 1/4 cup *(17 g)* chives, finely chopped
- 1/2 cup *(120 ml)* almond or coconut milk
- Salt and pepper to taste
- 8 slices of prosciutto or bacon (optional)

instructions

1. Preheat the oven to 350 F *(175 C)*.
2. Whisk the eggs and add in the chopped kale and chives. Also add in the almond/coconut milk, salt, and pepper. Mix well.
3. Grease 8 muffin cups with coconut oil or line each cup with a prosciutto slice.
4. Divide the egg mixture between the 8 muffin cups. Fill only 2/3 of each cup as the mixture rises when it's baking.
5. Bake in oven for 30 minutes.
6. Let cool a few minutes and then lift out carefully with a fork. Note that the muffins will sink a bit.

the Essential
KETO
COOKBOOK

BREAKFAST TURKEY WRAP

Prep Time: 5 minutes | **Cook Time:** 20 minutes | **Total Time:** 25 minutes
Yield: 1 serving
Nutritional Data (estimates) - per serving:
Calories: 360   Fat: 30 g   Net Carbohydrates: 3 g   Protein: 20 g

ingredients

- 2 slices of turkey breast (use more if the slices break easily)
- 2 romaine lettuce leaves (or 2 slices of avocado)
- 2 slices of bacon
- 2 eggs
- 1 Tablespoon *(15 ml)* coconut oil to cook in

instructions

1. Cook the 2 slices of bacon to the crispness you like.
2. Scramble the 2 eggs in the coconut oil (or bacon fat).
3. Make 2 wraps by placing half the scrambled eggs, 1 slice of bacon, and 1 romaine lettuce leaf on each slice of turkey breast.

EASY BACON CUPS

Prep Time: 15 minutes | **Cook Time:** 25 minutes | **Total Time:** 40 minutes
Yield: 4 servings
Nutritional Data (estimates) - per serving:
Calories: 180   Fat: 18 g   Net Carbohydrates: 0 g   Protein: 5 g

ingredients
- 20 thin slices of bacon
- Equipment: standard nonstick metal muffin or cupcake pan

instructions
1. Preheat oven to 400 F *(200 C)*.
2. Each bacon cup will require 2 and 1/2 slices of bacon.
3. Start by turning the entire muffin/cupcake pan over, so that the side that is normally the bottom is on top. To make 1 bacon cup, place 2 half slices of bacon across the back of one of the muffin/cupcake cups, both in the same direction. Then, place another half slice across those 2, perpendicular to the direction of the first 2 half slices. Finally, wrap a whole slice of bacon tightly around the sides of the cup. The slice wrapped around the sides will help to hold the bottom pieces of bacon together.
4. Repeat Step #3 for the other cups.
5. Place the entire pan *(still upside-down)* into the oven and bake for 25 minutes until crispy *(place a baking tray underneath in the oven to catch any dripping bacon fat)*.

Fill these bacon cups up with some guacamole, a poached egg, or scrambled eggs

KETO

Appetizers

CHAPTER 2

CHICKEN NOODLE SOUP

Prep Time: 15 minutes | **Cook Time:** 15 minutes | **Total Time:** 30 minutes
Yield: 2 servings
Nutritional Data (estimates) - per serving:
Calories: 310   Fat: 16 g   Net Carbohydrates: 4 g   Protein: 34 g

ingredients

- 3 cups *(720 ml)* chicken broth or bone broth
- 1 chicken breast *(approx 225 g or 0.5 lb)*, chopped into small pieces
- 2 Tablespoons *(30 ml)* avocado oil
- 1 stalk of celery, chopped
- 1 green onion, chopped
- 1/4 cup *(8 g)* cilantro, finely chopped
- 1 zucchini, peeled
- Salt to taste

instructions

1. Add the avocado oil into a saucepan and saute the diced chicken in there until cooked.
2. Add chicken broth to the same saucepan and simmer.
3. Add the chopped celery and green onion into the saucepan.
4. Create zucchini noodles – I used a potato peeler to create long strands, but other options include using a spiralizer or a food processor with the shredding attachment.
5. Add zucchini noodles and finely chopped cilantro to the saucepan. Simmer for a few more minutes, add salt to taste, and serve immediately.

Other options for keto noodles include long slices of cucumbers, shirataki noodles, and kelp noodles.

the Essential
KETO

BACON WRAPPED CHICKEN BITES WITH GARLIC MAYO

Prep Time: 10 minutes | **Cook Time:** 30 minutes | **Total Time**: 40 minutes
Yield: 4 servings
Nutritional Data (estimates) - per serving:
Calories: 280   Fat: 25 g   Net Carbohydrates: 7 g   Protein: 7 g

ingredients

- 1 large chicken breast *(approx 225 g or 0.5 lb)*, cut into small bites (approx. 22-27 pieces)
- 8-9 thin slices of bacon, cut into thirds
- 3 Tablespoons *(30 g)* garlic powder

For the garlic mayo:

- 1/4 cup *(60 ml)* mayo (see page 125 for recipe)
- 2 cloves of garlic, minced
- Dash of salt
- Dash of chili powder (optional)
- 1 teaspoon *(5 ml)* lemon juice (optional)
- 1 teaspoon *(4 g)* garlic powder (optional)

instructions

1. Preheat oven to 400 F *(200 C)* and line a baking tray with foil.
2. Place the garlic power into a small bowl and dip each small chunk of chicken in it.
3. Wrap each short bacon piece around each garlic powder-dipped piece of chicken. Place the bacon wrapped chicken bites on the baking tray. (Try to space them out so they're not touching on the tray.)
4. Bake for 25-30 minutes until the bacon turns crispy.
5. Meanwhile, combine the garlic mayo ingredients in a small bowl and use a fork to whisk it slightly.
6. Serve the bacon wrapped chicken bites with cocktail sticks and the garlic mayo.

FIERY BUFFALO WINGS

Prep Time: 15 minutes | **Cook Time:** 45 minutes | **Total Time**: 1 hour
Yield: 4 servings
Nutritional Data (estimates) - per serving:
Calories: 500   Fat: 38 g   Net Carbohydrates: 3 g   Protein: 29

ingredients
- 12 small chicken wings
- 1/2 cup *(56 g)* coconut flour
- 1/2 teaspoon *(1 g)* cayenne pepper
- 1/2 teaspoon *(1 g)* black pepper
- 1/2 teaspoon *(1 g)* crushed red pepper flakes
- 1 Tablespoon *(7 g)* paprika
- 1 Tablespoon *(8 g)* garlic powder
- 1 Tablespoon *(15 g)* salt
- 1/4 cup *(60 ml)* ghee, melted
- 1/4 cup *(60 ml)* hot sauce

instructions
1. Preheat oven to 400 F *(200 C)*.
2. Mix the coconut flour, dried spices, and salt together in a bowl.
3. Coat each chicken wing with the coconut flour mixture. Refrigerate for 15-30 minutes to help the flour stick a bit better to the wings *(optional)*.
4. Grease a baking tray *(or line it with aluminum foil)*.
5. Mix the ghee and the hot sauce together well.
6. Dip each chicken wing into the ghee and hot sauce mixture and place onto the baking tray.
7. Bake for 45 minutes.

EASY EGG DROP SOUP

Prep Time: 5 minutes | **Cook Time:** 10 minutes | **Total Time:** 15 minutes
Yield: 1 serving
Nutritional Data (estimates) - per serving:
Calories: 130   Fat: 5 g   Net Carbohydrates: 5 g   Protein: 15 g

ingredients

- 2 cups *(480 ml)* chicken broth or bone broth
- 1/4 cup *(17 g)* scallions (chopped green onions)
- 1/2 tomato, sliced
- 1 egg, whisked
- 1 Tablespoon *(15 ml)* tamari sauce
- 1/2 teaspoon *(1 g)* fresh ginger, grated (optional)
- Salt and pepper to taste

instructions

1. Heat up the chicken broth *(or other broth)* in a saucepan.
2. Slowly drizzle in whisked egg and stir slowly clockwise until ribbons form.
3. Add in rest of ingredients and let it cook for a few minutes.

CRAB HASH WITH GINGER AND CILANTRO

Prep Time: 10 minutes | **Cook Time:** 15 minutes | **Total Time:** 25 minutes
Yield: 4-6 servings
Nutritional Data (estimates) - per serving:
Calories: 150   Fat: 7 g   Net Carbohydrates: 2 g   Protein: 19 g

ingredients

- 2 zucchinis, peeled and shredded
- 1 lb *(454 g)* lump crabmeat (fresh or canned)
- 1/4 cup *(17 g)* scallions (green onions) chopped (optional)
- 1/4 cup *(8 g)* cilantro, finely chopped
- 2 cloves of garlic, minced
- 2 teaspoons *(4 g)* fresh ginger, grated
- 1 Tablespoon *(15 ml)* lemon juice
- 2 boiled eggs, diced (optional)
- Salt to taste
- 2 Tablespoons *(30 ml)* coconut oil

instructions

1. Place 2 Tablespoons of coconut oil into a frying pan *(or a saucepan)*.
2. Add in the shredded zucchinis, crabmeat, and scallions and sauté for 5-10 minutes.
3. Lastly, add the cilantro, garlic, ginger, lemon juice, and salt to taste. Sauté for a few minutes more to combine the flavors.
4. Top with the diced boiled eggs (optional) and serve immediately.

substitutions

- Chicken breast *(finely diced)* can be used instead of crabmeat, but you should cook it separately first.
- Scrambled eggs can be used instead of boiled eggs.
- Apple cider vinegar can be used instead of lemon juice.

BIG EASY SALAD

Prep Time: 15 minutes | *Cook Time:* 0 minutes | *Total Time:* 15 minutes
Yield: 2 servings
Nutritional Data (estimates) - per serving:
Calories: 570   Fat: 36 g   Net Carbohydrates: 10 g   Protein: 40 g

ingredients

- 2 romaine lettuce, chopped into small pieces
- 10 cherry or grape tomatoes
- 1 Tablespoon *(4 g)* sliced almonds (optional)
- 4-6 slices of bacon, cooked (crumbled)
- 1/2 lb *(225 g)* ham, diced
- Olive oil and lemon juice as dressing

instructions

1. Add all the ingredients together and toss with olive oil and small amount of lemon juice to taste.

ASIAN DEVILED EGGS

Prep Time: 10 minutes | *Cook Time:* 10 minutes | *Total Time:* 20 minutes
Yield: 16 servings
Nutritional Data (estimates) - per serving:
Calories: 93   Fat: 8 g   Net Carbohydrates: 0 g   Protein: 6 g

ingredients

- 16 eggs
- 1 Tablespoon *(15 ml)* sesame oil
- 3 Tablespoons *(45 ml)* avocado oil
- 3 Tablespoons *(45 ml)* tamari sauce
- 1 teaspoon *(5 ml)* mustard
- 2 Tablespoons chives, finely diced
- 1 red chili pepper, finely sliced

instructions

1. Soft boil the eggs.
2. Slice each egg in half lengthwise.
3. Remove the yolks and set aside in a bowl. Mash or blend the yolks with the sesame oil, avocado oil, tamari sauce, and mustard.
4. Place the yolk mixture back into the egg whites (use piping bags or a small spoon).
5. Sprinkle the chives on top of the egg halves and place one slice of red chili pepper on top of each deviled egg half.

the Essential
KETO
COOKBOOK

RED CABBAGE SOUP

Prep Time: 15 minutes | **Cook Time:** 25 minutes | **Total Time:** 40 minutes
Yield: 8 servings
Nutritional Data (estimates) - per serving:
Calories: 128   Fat: 10 g   Net Carbohydrates: 4 g   Protein: 2 g

ingredients

- 1 red cabbage, sliced
- 1/4 onion, chopped
- 4 stalks of celery, chopped
- 1 bell pepper, chopped
- 8 cups *(2 l)* chicken broth or bone broth
- 2 tomatoes, chopped
- 3 Tablespoons *(45 ml)* avocado oil, to cook with
- 1/4 cup bacon bits *(optional)*
- Salt and pepper, to taste

instructions

1. Add avocado oil to a large pot and then saute the cabbage, onions, celery, and bell pepper for 3 minutes on high heat.
2. Pour in the broth and add in the chopped tomatoes.
3. Bring to a boil and then simmer for 20 minutes until the cabbage is tender. Season with salt and pepper, to taste, and top with some bacon bits (optional).

the Essential
KETO
COOKBOOK

HEARTY CAULIFLOWER, LEEK & BACON SOUP

Prep Time: 10 minutes | **Cook Time:** 1 hour | **Total Time:** 1 hour 10 minutes
Yield: 4 servings
Nutritional Data (estimates) - per serving:
Calories: 110   Fat: 4 g   Net Carbohydrates: 6 g   Protein: 10 g

ingredients
- 1/2 head of cauliflower, chopped
- 6 cups *(1.4 l)* chicken broth or bone broth
- 1 leek, chopped
- 5 slices of bacon, cooked
- Salt and pepper to taste

instructions
1. Place the chopped cauliflower and leek into a pot with the chicken broth.
2. Cover the pot and simmer for 1 hour or until tender.
3. Use an immersion blender to puree the vegetables to create a smooth soup. *(If you don't have an immersion blender, you can take the vegetables out, let cool briefly, puree in a normal blender, and then put back into the pot.)*
4. Crumble the cooked bacon into small pieces and drop into the soup.
5. Add salt and pepper to taste.

substitutions
- Onion can be used instead of leek *(use 1 small white or yellow onion).*

the Essential
KETO
COOKBOOK

ITALIAN TUNA SALAD

Prep Time: 10 minutes | *Cook Time:* 0 minutes | *Total Time:* 10 minutes
Yield: 2 servings
Nutritional Data (estimates) - per serving:
Calories: 330   Fat: 15 g   Net Carbohydrates: 3 g   Protein: 43 g

ingredients

- 10 cherry tomatoes (or 5 sun-dried tomatoes), chopped
- 2 *(5 oz or 140 g)* cans of tuna, drained and flaked
- 1-2 ribs of celery, finely diced
- 1 clove of garlic, minced
- 3 Tablespoons *(6 g)* parsley, finely chopped
- 1/2 Tablespoon *(7 ml)* lemon juice
- 2 Tablespoons *(30 ml)* olive oil
- Salt and pepper to taste

instructions

1. Mix all ingredients together in a bowl and serve.

BROCCOLI BACON SALAD

Prep Time: 10 minutes | *Cook Time:* 30 minutes | *Total Time:* 40 minutes
Yield: 6 servings
Nutritional Data (estimates) - per serving:
Calories: 280   Fat: 26 g   Net Carbohydrates: 5 g   Protein: 7 g

ingredients

- 1 lb *(454 g)* broccoli florets
- 4 small red onions or 2 large ones, sliced
- 20 slices of bacon, chopped into small pieces
- 1 cup *(240 ml)* coconut milk or 1/2 cup *(120 ml)* coconut ranch dressing (see page 128 for recipe)
- Salt to taste

instructions

1. Cook the bacon first, and then cook the onions in the bacon fat.
2. Blanche the broccoli florets (or you can use them raw or soften them by boiling them first).
3. Toss the bacon pieces, onions, and broccoli florets together with the coconut milk and salt to taste. Serve at room temperature.

the Essential
KETO

Chicken Entrees

CHAPTER 3A

GRILLED CHICKEN SKEWERS WITH GARLIC SAUCE

Prep Time: 15 minutes | **Cook Time:** 15 minutes | **Total Time:** 30 minutes
Yield: 2 servings
Nutritional Data (estimates) - per serving:
Calories: 580   Fat: 33 g   Net Carbohydrates: 9 g   Protein: 55 g

ingredients

For the skewers:
- 1 lb *(454 g)* chicken breast, cut into large cubes (approx 1-inch)
- 1 onion, chopped
- 2 bell peppers, chopped
- 1 zucchini

For the garlic sauce:
- 1 head of garlic, peeled
- 1 teaspoon *(5 g)* salt
- Approx. 1/4 cup *(60 ml)* lemon juice
- Approx. 1 cup *(240 ml)* olive oil

For the marinade:
- 1/2 cup *(120 ml)* olive oil
- 1 teaspoon *(5 g)* salt

instructions

1. Heat up the grill to high. If using wooden skewers, soak them in water first.
2. For the garlic sauce, place the garlic cloves and salt into the blender. Then add in around 1/8 cup of the lemon juice and 1/2 cup of olive oil.
3. Blend well for 5-10 seconds, then slow your blender down and drizzle in more lemon juice and olive oil alternatively until it forms a smooth consistency.
4. Keep half the garlic sauce to serve with.
5. Take the other half of the garlic sauce and add in the additional 1/2 cup of olive oil and teaspoon of salt. Mix well - this makes the marinade.
6. Chop the chicken, onion, bell peppers, and zucchini into approximate 1-inch cubes or squares. Mix them in a bowl with the marinade.
7. Place the cubes on skewers and grill on high until the chicken is cooked (usually, we grill on the bottom for a few minutes to get the charred look and then move the skewers to a top rack with the lid down to cook the chicken well).
8. Serve with the garlic sauce you kept.

SPINACH BASIL CHICKEN MEATBALLS

Prep Time: 10 minutes | **Cook Time:** 15 minutes | **Total Time:** 25 minutes
Yield: 2 servings
Nutritional Data (estimates) - per serving:
Calories: 600   Fat: 40 g   Net Carbohydrates: 4 g   Protein: 55 g

ingredients
- 2 chicken breasts *(approx. 1 lb or 454 g)*
- 1/4 lb *(115 g)* spinach
- 2 teaspoons *(10 g)* salt
- 10 basil leaves
- 5 cloves of garlic, peeled
- 3 Tablespoons *(45 ml)* olive oil
- 2 Tablespoons *(30 ml)* olive oil or avocado oil to cook in

instructions
1. Place the chicken breasts, spinach, salt, basil leaves, garlic, and 3 Tablespoons of olive oil into a food processor and process well.
2. Make ping-pong ball sized meatballs from the meat mixture.
3. Add the 2 Tablespoons olive oil or avocado oil to a frying pan and fry the meatballs for 4 minutes on medium heat (fry in 2 batches if necessary). Turn the meatballs and fry for another 10 minutes. Make sure the meatballs don't get burnt.
4. Check the meatballs are fully cooked by cutting into one or using a meat thermometer.

These are great as an appetizer or as an entree, and it's a fantastic way to get more spinach into your diet. Serve with some garlic sauce (see page 131 for recipe) or by themselves.

THAI CHICKEN AND "RICE"

Prep Time: 10 minutes | ***Cook Time:*** 15 minutes | ***Total Time:*** 25 minutes
Yield: 4 servings
Nutritional Data (estimates) - per serving:
Calories: 480   Fat: 31 g   Net Carbohydrates: 4 g   Protein: 41 g

ingredients
- 1 head of cauliflower
- Meat from a small roasted chicken (or use 3 cooked chicken breasts), shredded (or use some leftover meat)
- 2 eggs, whisked
- 1 Tablespoon *(5 g)* fresh ginger, grated
- 3 cloves of garlic, minced
- 1 Tablespoon *(15 ml)* tamari sauce
- 1/2 cup *(16 g)* cilantro, chopped
- 4 Tablespoons *(60 ml)* coconut oil to cook with
- Salt and pepper to taste

instructions
1. If you don't have cooked shredded chicken, poach 3 chicken breasts and shred them or use another leftover meat.
2. Break the cauliflower into florets and food process until it forms a rice-like texture (may need to be done in batches). Squeeze excess water out.
3. Scramble 2 eggs in some coconut oil. Lightly salt the scrambled eggs and put aside while you make the cauliflower rice.
4. Place the cauliflower "rice" into a large pan with coconut oil and cook the cauliflower rice (may need to be done in 2 pans or in batches). Keep the heat on medium and stir regularly for 10 minutes.
5. Add in the shredded chicken, scrambled eggs, ginger, garlic, tamari sauce, cilantro, salt, and pepper to taste. Mix together, cook for another 2-3 minutes and serve.

PAN-FRIED ITALIAN CHICKEN TENDERS

Prep Time: 15 minutes | **Cook Time:** 15 minutes | **Total Time:** 30 minutes
Yield: 2 servings
Nutritional Data (estimates) - per serving:
Calories: 600   Fat: 35 g   Net Carbohydrates: 3 g   Protein: 55 g

ingredients
- 1 lb *(454 g)* chicken tenders (approx. 12 chicken tenders)
- 2/3 cup *(160 ml)* olive oil + more for cooking
- 2 Tablespoons *(30 ml)* lime juice or white wine vinegar
- 1.5 Tablespoons *(20 g)* mustard
- 2 teaspoons *(2 g)* Italian seasoning (see page 129 for recipe)
- 4 cloves of garlic
- 1 teaspoon *(5 g)* salt and to taste
- Salad leaves

instructions
1. Place the olive oil, lime juice or vinegar, mustard, Italian seasoning, garlic, and 1 teaspoon salt into the blender and blend well.
2. Heat up a frying pan and place 2 Tablespoons of olive oil into it. Place half the chicken tenders into the pan and cook on medium to high heat. Add in 1/3 of the mixture from the blender into the frying pan, coating the chicken tenders.
3. After 3-4 minutes, flip the chicken tenders (they should be browned) and cook the other side for 2-3 minutes until done. Test using a meat thermometer or cut one open to see if the chicken is cooked through. Repeat for the rest of the chicken tenders (if you have 2 frying pans, you can cook both batches simultaneously).
4. Divide the salad between 2 plates and place 6 cooked chicken tenders on top of each salad. Serve with the rest of the sauce from the blender.

CHICKEN NUGGETS

Prep Time: 10 minutes | *Cook Time:* 15 minutes | *Total Time:* 25 minutes
Yield: 2 servings
Nutritional Data (estimates) - per serving:
Calories: 550   Fat: 27 g   Net Carbohydrates: 8 g   Protein: 60 g

ingredients
- 2 chicken breasts, cut into cubes
- 1/2 cup *(56 g)* coconut flour
- 1 egg
- 2 Tablespoons *(20 g)* garlic powder
- 1 teaspoon *(5 g)* salt *(or to taste)*
- 1/4-1/2 cup *(60-120 ml)* ghee for shallow frying

instructions
1. Cube the chicken breasts if you haven't done so already.
2. In a bowl, mix together the coconut flour, garlic powder, and salt. Taste the mixture to see if you'd like more salt.
3. In a separate bowl, whisk 1 egg to make the egg wash.
4. Place the ghee in a saucepan on medium heat *(or use a deep fryer)*.
5. Dip the cubed chicken in the egg wash and then drop into the coconut flour mixture to coat it with the "breading."
6. Carefully place some of the "breaded" chicken cubes into the ghee and fry until golden *(approx. 10 minutes)*. Make sure there's only a single layer of chicken in the pan so that they can all cook in the oil. Turn the chicken pieces to make sure they get cooked uniformly. Depending on the size of the pan, you might need to do this step in batches.
7. Place the cooked chicken pieces onto paper towels to soak up any excess oil. Enjoy by themselves or with some coconut ranch dressing (see page 128 for recipe) or garlic sauce (see page 131 for recipe).

COCONUT CHICKEN CURRY

Prep Time: 15 minutes | **Cook Time:** 50 minutes | **Total Time:** 1 hour 5 minutes
Yield: 4 servings
Nutritional Data (estimates) - per serving:
Calories: 450   Fat: 25 g   Net Carbohydrates: 9 g   Protein: 45 g

ingredients

- 3 chicken breasts, cut into chunks
- 1 Tablespoon *(15 ml)* ghee or coconut oil
- 1 cup *(240 ml)* coconut cream (the top layer of cream from a refrigerated can of coconut milk)
- 1 cup *(240 ml)* chicken broth
- 2 cups *(250 g)* carrots (or zucchini), diced
- 1 cup *(100 g)* celery, chopped
- 2 tomatoes, diced
- 1 Tablespoon *(5 g)* fresh ginger, grated
- 1.5 Tablespoons *(10 g)* curry powder or garam masala
- 1/4 cup *(8 g)* cilantro, roughly chopped
- 6 cloves of garlic, minced
- Salt to taste

instructions

1. Sauté the chicken in the ghee in a medium-sized saucepan.
2. When the outside of the chicken has all turned white, add in the coconut cream and the chicken broth and mix well.
3. Add in the carrots, celery, and tomatoes.
4. Add in the ginger and curry powder (or garam masala).
5. Cook on medium heat with the lid on for 40 minutes (stirring occasionally).
6. Add in the cilantro, minced garlic, and salt to taste. Cook for another 5 minutes and serve. Enjoy by itself, with a slice of Microwave Quick Bread (see page 101 for recipe), or with some Cauliflower White "Rice" (see page 99 for recipe).

PRESSURE COOKER CHICKEN STEW

Prep Time: 15 minutes | **Cook Time:** 35 minutes | **Total Time:** 50 minutes
Yield: 3 servings
Nutritional Data (estimates) - per serving:
Calories: 250   Fat: 4 g   Net Carbohydrates: 4 g   Protein: 44 g

ingredients

- 2-3 chicken breasts *(approx. 1 lb or 454 g)*, diced
- 4 cups *(1 l)* chicken broth or bone broth
- 2 small carrots, chopped
- 3 stalks of celery, chopped
- 1/2 onion, chopped
- 1 teaspoon *(5 ml)* tamari sauce
- 1/2 Tablespoon *(1 g)* fresh thyme leaves *(or use 1/2 tsp (0.5 g) dried thyme)*
- 1/2 cup *(15 g)* parsley, chopped and divided (save half for when you're serving)
- 1 Tablespoon *(7 g)* unflavored gelatin powder (optional)
- Salt to taste

instructions

1. Place the diced chicken breasts, chicken broth, chopped carrots, chopped celery, chopped onion, tamari sauce, thyme, and half the parsley into the pressure cooker pot.
2. If you're adding in gelatin, then stir it in until it dissolves.
3. Set the pressure cooker on high pressure for 35 minutes. When ready, follow your pressure cooker's instructions for releasing the pressure safely.
4. Add salt to taste and sprinkle in the rest of the chopped parsley.

CHICKEN BACON BURGERS

Prep Time: 10 minutes | **Cook Time**: 15 minutes | **Total Time:** 25 minutes
Yield: 8 servings
Nutritional Data (estimates) - per serving:
Calories: 319   Fat: 24 g   Net Carbohydrates: 1 g   Protein: 25 g

ingredients
- 4 chicken breasts
- 4 slices of bacon
- 1/4 medium onion
- 2 cloves of garlic
- 1/4 cup *(60 ml)* avocado oil, to cook with

instructions
1. Food process the chicken, bacon, onion and garlic and form 8 patties. You might need to do this in batches.
2. Fry patties in the avocado oil in batches. Make sure burgers are fully cooked.
3. Serve with guacamole (see page 131 for recipe).

BASIL CHICKEN SAUTE

Prep Time: 10 minutes | **Cook Time:** 15 minutes | **Total Time:** 25 minutes
Yield: 2 servings
Nutritional Data (estimates) - per serving:
Calories: 320   Fat: 24 g   Net Carbohydrates: 2 g   Protein: 24 g

ingredients
- 1 chicken breast *(0.5 lb or 225 g)*, minced or chopped very small
- 2 cloves of garlic, minced
- 1 chili pepper, diced *(optional)*
- 1 cup *(1 large bunch)* basil leaves, finely chopped
- 1 Tablespoon *(15 ml)* tamari sauce
- 2 Tablespoons *(30 ml)* avocado or coconut oil to cook in
- Salt, to taste

instructions
1. Add oil to a frying pan and saute the garlic and pepper.
2. Then add in the minced chicken and saute until the chicken is cooked.
3. Add the tamari sauce and salt to taste. Add in the basil leaves and mix it in.

the Essential
KETO
COOKBOOK

SINGAPORE-STYLE NOODLES

Prep Time: 10 minutes | *Cook Time:* 15 minutes | *Total Time:* 25 minutes
Yield: 4 servings
Nutritional Data (estimates) - per serving:
Calories: 370   Fat: 24 g   Net Carbohydrates: 6 g   Protein: 29 g

ingredients

- 3 Tablespoons *(45 ml)* avocado oil, to cook with
- 2 zucchinis, shredded (squeeze out as much moisture from it as possible)
- 1 carrot, shredded (squeeze out as much moisture from it as possible)
- 1/2 onion, diced
- 3 eggs, whisked
- 1 chicken breast, diced (or replace with beef or shrimp)
- 3 cloves garlic, peeled and minced
- 1 teaspoon fresh ginger, minced
- 1 red bell pepper, thinly sliced (use chili peppers if you like it spicy)
- 1 Tablespoon *(6 g)* curry powder
- 2 Tablespoons *(30 ml)* gluten-free tamari sauce or coconut aminos
- 1 Tablespoon *(15 ml)* apple cider vinegar

instructions

1. Add the avocado oil to a hot pan and saute the diced chicken breast until cooked. Remove from the pan and set aside. Then add in the eggs and scramble until mostly cooked.

2. Add in the vegetables to the pan along with the spices, seasoning, and apple cider vinegar. Then add the chicken breast back in and cook for 5 more minutes.

SLOW COOKER JERK CHICKEN

Prep Time: 10 minutes | ***Cook Time***: 5 hours | ***Total Time***: 5 hours 10 minutes
Yield: 4 servings
Nutritional Data (estimates) - per serving:
Calories: 480   Fat: 30 g   Net Carbohydrates: 4 g   Protein: 45 g

ingredients

- 8 chicken drumsticks and 8 chicken wings
- 4 teaspoons *(20 g)* salt
- 4 teaspoons *(9 g)* paprika
- 1 teaspoon *(2 g)* cayenne pepper
- 2 teaspoons *(5 g)* onion powder
- 2 teaspoons *(3 g)* dried thyme
- 2 teaspoons *(4 g)* white pepper
- 2 teaspoons *(6 g)* garlic powder
- 1 teaspoon *(2 g)* black pepper

instructions

1. Mix all the spices together in a bowl to make a rub for the chicken.
2. Wash the chicken meat in cold water briefly. Place the washed chicken meat into the bowl with the rub, and rub the spices onto the meat thoroughly, including under the skin.
3. Place each piece of chicken covered with the spices into the slow cooker (*no liquid required*).
4. Set the slow cooker on medium heat, and cook for 5 hours or until the chicken meat falls off the bone.

If you've got some cajun seasoning handy (see page 129 for recipe), then use that for this recipe to make it even easier.

CRISPY CHICKEN DRUMSTICKS

Prep Time: 5 minutes | **Cook Time**: 40 minutes | **Total Time:** 45 minutes
Yield: 2 servings
Nutritional Data (estimates) - per serving:
Calories: 630   Fat: 33 g   Net Carbohydrates: 4 g   Protein: 72 g

ingredients

- 10 chicken drumsticks
- 1-2 *(15-30 g)* Tablespoons salt
- 3 Tablespoons *(24 g)* curry powder (or onion powder)
- 3 Tablespoons *(30 g)* garlic powder
- 1/2 Tablespoon *(7 ml)* of coconut oil for greasing baking tray (optional)

instructions

1. Preheat oven to 450 F *(230 C)*. Grease a large baking tray with coconut oil.
2. Mix the salt and spices together in a bowl.
3. Coat each drumstick with the mixture, place on the baking tray, and bake for 40 minutes.

Beef Entrees

CHAPTER 3B

OLD FASHIONED LASAGNA

Prep Time: 15 minutes | *Cook Time:* 1 hour 50 minutes
Total Time: 2 hours 5 minutes | *Yield:* 8 servings
Nutritional Data (estimates) - per serving:
Calories: 300   Fat: 19 g   Net Carbohydrates: 10 g   Protein: 20 g

ingredients

- 3/4 lb *(341 g)* ground pork *(or other meat)*
- 3/4 lb *(341 g)* ground beef *(or other meat)*
- 1 small onion, finely chopped
- 1 28-ounce *(794 g)* can diced tomatoes
- 2 6-ounce *(170 g)* cans of tomato paste
- 2 Tablespoons *(5 g)* fresh basil, diced
- 6 Tablespoons *(23 g)* fresh parsley, diced
- 1 Tablespoon *(3 g)* fresh oregano, diced
- 1 Tablespoon *(3 g)* fresh thyme, diced
- 1 teaspoon *(2 g)* fennel seeds
- 4 cloves of garlic, minced
- 2 eggs, whisked
- 2 Tablespoons *(30 ml)* coconut oil
- Salt to taste
- 1 large eggplant, sliced into thin slices
- 3 Tablespoons *(45 g)* salt for boiling eggplants

instructions

1. Place 2 Tablespoons of coconut oil into a large stock pot. Add in the ground meat and the onion. Cook until the meat browns and the onion turns translucent.

2. Then add in the tomatoes, tomato paste, fresh herbs, fennel seeds, and minced garlic.

3. Cook on a low simmer with the lid on for 45 minutes. Stir regularly to make sure nothing sticks to the bottom of the pot.

4. Preheat the oven to 375 F *(190 C)* and boil a pot of water. Add the 3 Tablespoons of salt into the boiling water, then add in the eggplant slices. Boil for 2-3 minutes and then remove and place in cold water *(if your slices are thicker, then you might need to boil for longer - the eggplant should soften so that you can cut it with a fork fairly easily).*

5. Add the whisked eggs into the meat mixture and stir slowly to mix the eggs in. Cook the meat mixture for 10 minutes more and then add salt to taste.

6. Pour half the meat mixture into the bottom of a 13 by 9 inch lasagna pan or a similar baking pan. Top with half the eggplant slices.

7. Then pour the other half of the egg/meat mixture on top of the eggplant slices, and top that egg/meat layer with the rest of the eggplant slices.

8. Cover the tray with aluminum foil and bake for 45-50 minutes.

ZUCCHINI BEEF PHO

Prep Time: 15 minutes | **Cook Time:** 10 minutes | **Total Time:** 25 minutes
Yield: 2 servings
Nutritional Data (estimates) - per serving:
Calories: 300   Fat: 14 g   Net Carbohydrates: 7 g   Protein: 30 g

ingredients

- 3 cups *(720 ml)* chicken/beef broth *or* bone broth
- 1/2 lb *(225 g)* beef round, sliced very thin
- 1 teaspoon *(1 g)* fresh ginger, grated
(or use 1/2 teaspoon *(1 g)* ginger powder)
- 1/2 teaspoon *(1 g)* cinnamon powder
- 2 green onions, diced (scallions)
- 1/4 cup *(8 g)* cilantro, finely diced
- 2 zucchinis, shredded
(or 2 packs of shirataki noodles)
- Salt and pepper to taste
- 10 basil leaves
- 1/2 lime, cut into 4 wedges

A spiralizer can be a fun way to make noodles using zucchini or cucumber, but if you don't want to splash out for one of those devices, you can use a julienne peeler, a potato peeler, or your food processor's shredding attachment to make your noodle strands.

instructions

1. Slice the beef round very thinly against the grain (tip: freeze the beef for 20-30 minutes before slicing to get thinner slices).
2. Heat up the broth.
3. When the broth starts boiling, add in the freshly grated ginger, cinnamon powder, and salt and pepper to taste.
4. Add in the beef slices slowly, making sure they don't all clump together.
5. Then add in the zucchini noodles, the green onions, and the cilantro.
6. Cook for 1 minute until the beef slices are done.
7. Serve with the basil leaves and lime wedges.

MEXICAN TACOS

Prep Time: 15 minutes | **Cook Time:** 15 minutes | **Total Time:** 30 minutes
Yield: 2 servings
Nutritional Data (estimates) - per serving:
Calories: 560   Fat: 37 g   Net Carbohydrates: 7 g   Protein: 47 g

ingredients

Lettuce, deli meat, and store-bought coconut wraps (if you can find them) are all good options for wraps

- 1 lb *(454 g)* ground beef
- 1 small onion, diced
- 2 tomatoes, diced
- 1 bell pepper, diced
- 1 jalapeño pepper, deseeded and diced
- 2 cloves of garlic, minced
- 1 Tablespoon *(6 g)* cumin powder
- 1 Tablespoon *(6 g)* paprika
- 1 Tablespoon *(5 g)* dried oregano
- 1/4 teaspoon *(0.5 g)* chili powder *(or to taste)*
- Salt and pepper to taste
- 1/4 cup *(8 g)* cilantro, finely chopped *(for garnish)*
- 1 Tablespoon *(15 ml)* coconut oil to cook with
- Lettuce leaves to serve with

instructions

1. Sauté the onions in the coconut oil until the onions turn translucent.
2. Add in the ground beef and sauté until the beef is pretty much cooked *(turns light brown)*. Use a spatula to stir the beef to ensure it doesn't clump together. Pour out any excess water/oil produced during cooking.
3. When the beef is pretty much cooked, add in the tomatoes, bell pepper, jalapeño pepper, minced garlic, cumin powder, paprika, oregano, chili powder, salt, and pepper.
4. Cook until the tomatoes and peppers are soft.
5. Garnish with cilantro and serve with lettuce wraps or by themselves.

MINI BURGERS

Prep Time: 10 minutes | **Cook Time:** 20 minutes | **Total Time:** 30 minutes
Yield: 4 servings
Nutritional Data (estimates) - per serving:
Calories: 553   Fat: 52 g   Net Carbohydrates: 1 g   Protein: 21 g

INGREDIENTS
- 12 oz *(340 g)* ground beef
- 2 Tablespoons *(28 g)* mustard
- Pickles (optional)
- A few lettuce leaves
- Salt to taste
- 2 Tablespoons *(30 ml)* avocado oil (or coconut oil or ghee), to cook with

For "burger buns:"
- 2/3 cup *(70 g)* almond flour
- 1 teaspoon *(4 g)* baking powder
- 1 teaspoon *(5 g)* salt
- 2 eggs
- 5 Tablespoons *(75 ml)* avocado oil (or coconut oil or ghee), melted

INSTRUCTIONS
1. Make 4 small thin patties with the ground beef (each should be approx. 2-inch across in diameter).
2. Place avocado oil into a frying pan and fry the burger patties on medium to high heat. Fry for 2 minutes on each side until both sides are well browned (this is around medium in terms of rareness for the patties).
3. After the patties are cooked, salt them lightly and place them on a plate to drain.
4. Meanwhile, take 2 mugs and divide the burger bun ingredients between the 2 mugs (i.e., 1/3 cup almond flour, 1/2 teaspoon baking powder, 1/2 teaspoon salt, 1 egg, and 2.5 Tablespoons coconut oil in each mug). Mix well.
5. Microwave each mug for 90 seconds on high. Wait a few minutes before popping them out of the mug. Slice each bread into 4 slices and use as burger buns. (Gently fry them for a few seconds in the frying pan without oil for a toasted taste.)
6. Serve the burgers (1 mini burger for each person) with the mustard, lettuce leaves, and pickles.

SPAGHETTI BOLOGNESE BAKE

Prep Time: 15 minutes | **Cook Time:** 45 minutes | **Total Time:** 60 minutes
Yield: 8 servings
Nutritional Data (estimates) - per serving:
Calories: 392   Fat: 31 g   Net Carbohydrates: 5 g   Protein: 20 g

INGREDIENTS

- 2 lbs *(900 g)* ground beef
- 1/2 onion, diced
- 1/4 cup *(60 ml)* avocado oil, to cook with
- Salt and pepper, to taste
- 1 can *(400 g)* diced tomatoes
- 1/2 can *(200 g)* tomato sauce
- 3 cloves of garlic, finely diced or minced
- 2 zucchinis, spiralized, shredded, or peeled into long noodle-like strands
- 1/2 cup *(16 g)* fresh basil leaves, finely chopped

INSTRUCTIONS

1. Preheat oven to 350 F *(175 C)*.
2. Add the avocado oil to a hot pan and brown the beef and onions.
3. Add into a large baking dish with the rest of the ingredients (except the zucchinis and basil).
4. Bake for 30 minutes.
5. Then carefully stir in the zucchini noodles and basil, let sit for 5 minutes, and serve.

SPAGHETTI SQUASH BOLOGNESE

Prep Time: 10 minutes | ***Cook Time:*** 50 minutes | ***Total Time:*** 1 hour
Yield: 4 servings
Nutritional Data (estimates) - per serving:
Calories: 450   Fat: 30 g   Net Carbohydrates: 8 g   Protein: 45 g

ingredients
- 1 spaghetti squash
- 2 lb *(908 g)* ground or minced beef
- 1 large onion, diced
- 1 14.5 oz *(410 g)* can of diced tomatoes
- 1 cup *(40 g)* fresh basil, finely chopped
- 8 cloves of garlic, minced
- Coconut oil to cook with
- Salt and pepper to taste

instructions
1. Cook the onion in a large pot with coconut oil. Add the ground beef.
2. Once the meat is browned, add the diced tomatoes and simmer with the lid on for 30 minutes (simmer for 1 hour if you have time). Stir regularly to make sure it's not sticking to the bottom of the pot.
3. Meanwhile, chop a spaghetti squash in half, remove the seeds (you can roast the seeds for a snack), cover the insides with a thin layer of coconut oil (you can use your hands to do this), cover with a paper towel to avoid splattering, and microwave each half for 6-7 minutes on high.
4. Use a fork to scratch out the spaghetti squash strands and divide between 4 plates.
5. Add the basil, garlic, salt, and pepper to taste to the meat sauce, cook for 5 more minutes, and top onto the spaghetti squash.

MUSTARD GROUND BEEF SAUTE

Prep Time: 5 minutes | **Cook Time**: 15 minutes | **Total Time:** 20 minutes
Yield: 2 servings
Nutritional Data (estimates) - per serving:
Calories: 480   Fat: 30 g   Net Carbohydrates: 6 g   Protein: 40 g

ingredients

- 0.8 lbs *(360 g)* ground beef
- 5 celery stalks, cut into thin slices
- 10 cherry tomatoes, halved (or 1 tomato, chopped)
- 1 egg
- 1.5 Tablespoons *(20 g)* yellow mustard
- 6 cloves of garlic, minced
- Salt to taste
- 1 Tablespoon *(15 ml)* coconut oil to cook with

instructions

1. Melt the coconut oil in a large frying pan or saucepan on medium heat and cook the ground beef until all of it turns brown. Stir regularly to get it to cook evenly and to break up any large chunks.
2. Add in the celery slices and cherry tomato halves and cook for 5 minutes while stirring regularly.
3. Break an egg into the pan and stir to mix it into the ground beef mixture.
4. Add in the mustard and garlic, and cook until the pieces of eggs are cooked *(not liquid anymore)*.
5. Add salt, to taste.

The mustard makes this recipe amazing! In fact, it's one of our favorites.

the Essential
KETO
COOKBOOK

GUACAMOLE BURGERS

Prep Time: 10 minutes | ***Cook Time:*** 20 minutes | ***Total Time:*** 30 minutes
Yield: 4 servings
Nutritional Data (estimates) - per serving:
Calories: 600   Fat: 45 g   Net Carbohydrates: 4 g   Protein: 45 g

ingredients

- 1-1.5 lbs *(454-731 g)* ground beef
- 4 eggs
- Coconut oil to cook with
- 1 cup *(220 g)* guacamole (see page 131 for recipe)

instructions

1. With your hands, mold the ground beef into 4 patties.
2. Cook the 4 burger patties, either in a skillet with a bit of coconut oil or on a grill.
3. Once the burgers are cooked through, place to the side.
4. Fry the eggs *(preferably in coconut oil)* in a skillet.
5. Place 1 fried egg on top of each burger and then top with guacamole.

You can also use store-bought guacamole if you don't have time to make your own.

the Essential
KETO
COOKBOOK

SLOW COOKER ASIAN POT ROAST

Prep Time: 10 minutes | *Cook Time:* 8 hours | *Total Time:* 8 hours 10 minutes
Yield: 4 servings
Nutritional Data (estimates) - per serving:
Calories: 490   Fat: 23 g   Net Carbohydrates: 2 g   Protein: 63 g

ingredients
For the roast:
- 2 lbs (*908 g*) beef round roast
- 1 cup (*240 ml*) tamari sauce
- 1 cup (*240 ml*) beef broth
- 1-2 Tablespoons (*15-30 g*) salt (omit if beef broth is already salted)
- 1 Tablespoon (*7 g*) onion powder
- 1 Tablespoon (*10 g*) garlic powder
- 3-4 star anise
- 10 Szechuan peppercorns

For the sauce:
- 2 Tablespoons (*30 ml*) tamari sauce
- 1 teaspoon (*5 ml*) sesame oil
- 1 clove garlic, minced
- 1/4 teaspoon (*1 ml*) Chinese chili oil (optional)

instructions
1. Put all the roast ingredients into the slow cooker.
2. Fill the slow cooker with enough water to cover the meat (approximately 4 cups, but this will vary depending on the size of your slow cooker).
3. Cook in the slow cooker on low heat for 8 hours.
4. Take the meat out of the slow cooker without the brine and let it cool. Then place into the fridge.
5. Make the sauce by mixing all the sauce ingredients together in a small bowl.
6. To serve, cut the roast into thin slices and lightly drizzle the sauce over the slices.

You can make a large batch of this in advance and use in various stir-fries and sautes.

MARINATED GRILLED FLANK STEAK

Prep Time: 8 hrs *(for marinating)* | **Cook Time:** 30 minutes
Total Time: 8 hrs 30 minutes | **Yield:** 6 servings
Nutritional Data (estimates) - per serving:
Calories: 700 Fat: 50 g Net Carbohydrates: 4 g Protein: 50 g

ingredients
- 3 lbs *(1361 g)* flank steak
- 1 cup *(240 ml)* olive oil
- 2/3 cup *(160 ml)* tamari sauce
- 1/2 cup *(120 ml)* vinegar
- Juice from 1 lemon
- 2 Tablespoons *(28 g)* mustard
- 6 cloves of garlic, minced
- 1 Tablespoon *(5 g)* fresh ginger, grated *(or ginger powder)*
- 1 Tablespoon *(6 g)* paprika
- 1 Tablespoon *(7 g)* onion powder
- 1 Tablespoon *(15 g)* salt
- 2 teaspoons *(3 g)* dried thyme
- 1 teaspoon *(3 g)* chili powder

instructions
1. Chop the flank steak into manageable pieces if it's not already chopped.
2. Create the marinade by mixing all ingredients *(except the steak)* in a small bowl.
3. Place each piece of steak into a Ziploc bag and divide the marinade equally among the bags.
4. Seal the bags and marinate the steak overnight.
5. When ready, grill each steak by placing on a hot grill or skillet. Try to turn the steaks as little as possible. You can use a meat thermometer to get the steak to the level of rareness you desire. *(We found 3-4 minutes on each side on a hot 500-600 F grill with the lid down worked well.)*

the Essential
KETO
COOKBOOK

NO-PASTRY BEEF WELLINGTON

Prep Time: 30 minutes | **Cook Time:** 30 minutes | **Total Time:** 60 minutes
Yield: 2 servings
Nutritional Data (estimates) - per serving:
Calories: 580   Fat: 50 g   Net Carbohydrates: 2 g   Protein: 30 g

ingredients

For the duxelles:
- 3 large button mushrooms
- 1 Tablespoon *(10 g)* onions, chopped
- 1 teaspoon *(3 g)* garlic powder
- 1/2 teaspoon *(3 g)* salt
- 2 Tablespoons *(30 ml)* olive oil

Other ingredients:
- 1 9-ounce *(252 g)* filet mignon
- 8 thin slices of prosciutto (or 4 ham slices)
- 1 Tablespoon *(14 g)* yellow mustard
- 1/2 Tablespoon *(7 g)* salt
- 2 Tablespoons *(30 ml)* olive oil to cook in

instructions

1. Preheat oven to 400 F *(200 C)*.
2. Make the duxelles by blending the mushrooms, onions, garlic powder, salt, and olive oil together until pureed.
3. Then heat the mixture in a pan for 10 minutes on medium heat.
4. Place a large piece of cling-film onto the counter and place the slices of prosciutto side-by-side *(overlapping slightly)* to form a rectangular layer.
5. Spread the duxelles over the prosciutto layer.
6. Sprinkle the 1/2 Tablespoon of salt over the filet mignon.
7. Pan-sear the filet mignon in 2 Tablespoons of olive oil.
8. Spread the 1 Tablespoon of mustard on the seared filet mignon and place in the middle of the prosciutto and duxelles layer.
9. Use the cling-film to wrap the prosciutto around the filet mignon. Then wrap the cling-film around the package to secure it. Use a second piece of cling-film to pull the prosciutto-wrapped package tighter together. Refrigerate for 15 minutes.
10. Remove the cling-film from the refrigerated prosciutto-wrapped beef and place beef on a greased baking tray.
11. Bake for 20-25 minutes *(it should be pink when you cut into it)*.
12. To serve, carefully cut the Beef Wellington in half.

BEEF BACON STEW

Prep Time: 10 minutes | **Cook Time**: 2 hour 10 minutes
Total Time: 2 hour 20 minutes | **Servings:** 4 servings
Nutritional Data (estimates) - per serving:
Calories: 800   Fat: 50 g   Net Carbohydrates: 10 g   Protein: 75 g

ingredients

- 2 lbs *(908 g)* beef stew meat
- 1 carrot, peeled and diced
- 1/4 lb *(112 g)* green beans, chopped in half
- 1/2 pound *(225 g)* bacon, cooked and diced
- 8-12 cups *(1.9-2.8 l)* water or broth (so it covers the meat and vegetables)
- 3 Tablespoons *(21 g)* unflavored gelatin *(optional)*
- 3 Tablespoons *(18 g)* cumin powder
- 3 Tablespoons *(15 g)* dried onion flakes *(or substitute 1 chopped onion or onion powder)*
- 1 Tablespoon *(6 g)* turmeric
- 1 Tablespoon *(10 g)* garlic powder *(or substitute 3 cloves of garlic, minced)*
- 1 teaspoon *(1 g)* ginger powder *(or substitute 1 teaspoon freshly grated ginger)*
- Salt to taste

instructions

1. Add the beef, carrots, and green beans to the 8-12 cups (1.9-2.8 l) of water or broth in a large pot and bring to a boil. Then add in the gelatin and the spices and mix well. Place the lid on the pot and let simmer for 1 hour (simmer for 2 hours if you have time). Stir to make sure it doesn't stick to the bottom.
2. When the vegetables are soft, add in the cooked pieces of bacon.
3. Simmer for 5-10 minutes more.

the Essential
KETO

SLOW COOKER BEEF STEW

Prep Time: 10 minutes | *Cook Time:* 8 hours | *Total Time:* 8 hours 10 minutes
Yield: 6 servings
Nutritional Data (estimates) - per serving:
Calories: 380   Fat: 23 g   Net Carbohydrates: 3 g   Protein: 40 g

ingredients

- 2.5 lbs *(1.1 kg)* beef *(stew meat or short ribs meat)*
- 1 carrot, chopped
- 1 onion, chopped
- 4 celery sticks, chopped
- 2 cloves of garlic, minced
- 1 14.5-ounce *(406 ml)* can of broth *(beef, chicken, or vegetable)*
- 2 teaspoons *(10 g)* salt
- 1/2 teaspoon *(1 g)* black pepper
- 1 teaspoon *(3 g)* garlic powder
- 1 teaspoon *(2 g)* onion powder
- 2 teaspoons *(4 g)* paprika

instructions

1. Chop up the beef into 1-inch *(2.5 cm)* cubes if you're not using stew meat.
2. Pour the broth into the bottom of the slow cooker.
3. Place the meat into the slow cooker.
4. Add to the slow cooker the salt, pepper, garlic powder, onion powder, minced garlic, and paprika.
5. Then add the chopped vegetables to the slow cooker.
6. Place the lid on the slow cooker and cook on the low temperature setting for 8 hours.

BEEF CURRY

Prep Time: 15 minutes | *Cook Time:* 1 hour 16 minutes
Total Time: 1 hour 31 minutes | *Yield:* 4 servings
Nutritional Data (estimates) - per serving:
Calories: 440   Fat: 33 g   Net Carbohydrates: 7 g   Protein: 25 g

INGREDIENTS

- 1 lb *(454 g)* beef round, chopped into 1-inch cubes
- 1 onion, chopped
- 1 Tablespoon *(6 g)* curry powder
- 1 teaspoon *(2 g)* ground cumin
- 1 teaspoon *(2 g)* ground coriander
- 1 teaspoon *(2 g)* ground turmeric
- 1 teaspoon *(2 g)* cardamom
- 3/4 cup *(180 ml)* of coconut milk
- 2 carrots, diced
- 1 bell pepper, diced
- 10 button mushrooms, diced (optional)
- 1 Tablespoon *(15 ml)* fish sauce
- 1 teaspoon *(1 g)* fresh ginger, grated
- 2 cloves of garlic, minced
- 1/4 cup *(2 g)* fresh basil leaves, chopped
- Salt to taste
- Coconut oil to cook in

INSTRUCTIONS

1. In a saucepan, saute the beef and onions in 2 Tablespoons of coconut oil on medium heat for 5-6 minutes until the beef is browned.

2. Add the spices, coconut milk, carrots, bell pepper, mushrooms, and fish sauce. Bring to the boil, then cover and simmer for 1 hour until the beef is tender. Add some water if it gets too dry.

3. Add the chopped basil, garlic, ginger, and salt to taste and simmer for 10 more minutes.

4. Serve with some Cauliflower White "Rice" (see page 99 for recipe).

EASY BROCCOLI BEEF STIR-FRY

Prep Time: 10 minutes | **Cook Time:** 15 minutes | **Total Time:** 25 minutes
Yield: 2 servings
Nutritional Data (estimates) - per serving:
Calories: 400   Fat: 28 g   Net Carbohydrates: 6 g   Protein: 28 g

ingredients

- 2 cups *(225 g)* broccoli florets
- 1/2 lb *(225 g)* beef, sliced thin and precooked
(you can use leftover Slow Cooker Asian Pot Roast (see page 70 for recipe))
- 3 cloves of garlic, minced
- 1 teaspoon *(1 g)* fresh ginger, grated
- 2 Tablespoons *(30 ml)* tamari sauce or to taste
- Avocado oil to cook in

instructions

1. Place 2 Tablespoons of avocado oil into a skillet or saucepan on medium heat. Add the broccoli florets into the skillet.
2. When the broccoli softens to the amount you want (I like it soft, but some people like it crunchier), add in the beef slices.
3. Saute for 2 minutes and then add in the garlic, ginger, and tamari sauce.
4. Serve immediately.

Enjoy this classic Chinese dish with some Cauliflower White "Rice" (see page 99 for recipe)!

BIFTECK HACHE
(FRENCH HAMBURGERS)

Prep Time: 15 minutes | **Cook Time:** 15 minutes | **Total Time:** 30 minutes
Yield: 4 servings
Nutritional Data (estimates) - per serving:
Calories: 460   Fat: 36 g   Net Carbohydrates: 1 g   Protein: 35 g

ingredients

- 2 Tablespoons *(30 ml)* ghee or coconut oil, slightly melted
- 1 onion, finely diced (divided into 2 portions)
- 1.5 lb *(680 g)* ground beef
- 1 egg
- 1 Tablespoon *(2 g)* fresh thyme leaves
- Salt and pepper to taste
- Additional ghee or coconut oil to cook with

For the sauce:
- 1/2 cup *(120 ml)* beef stock
- 2 Tablespoons *(30 ml)* additional ghee
- 1/4 cup *(8 g)* parsley, finely chopped

This delicious recipe is based on Julia Child's original bifteck hache recipe published in Mastering the Art of French Cooking Volume 1.

instructions

1. Place the 2 Tablespoons of ghee or coconut oil into a frying pan and cook half the diced onions in the pan until they turn translucent.
2. Let the onions cool and then add them (including the oil in the pan) to a mixing bowl with the ground beef, egg, thyme leaves, salt, and pepper.
3. Mix well and form 8 patties from the meat mixture.
4. Cook the patties in a frying pan with additional ghee or coconut oil until both sides are well browned (make flatter patties if you prefer the burgers to be well-done).
5. For the sauce, pour out the remaining oil from the pan, add in the 2 Tablespoons of additional ghee and saute the rest of the diced onions. Then add in the beef stock and reduce the sauce down for a few minutes. Add in the parsley and serve the sauce with the burgers.

Pork Entrees

CHAPTER 3C

PRESSURE COOKER PORK SHOULDER

Prep Time: 10 minutes | **Cook Time:** 1 hour | **Total Time:** 1 hour 10 minutes
Yield: 2 servings
Nutritional Data (estimates) - per serving:
Calories: 550   Fat: 41 g   Net Carbohydrates: 1 g   Protein: 40 g

ingredients
- 1 lb *(454 g)* pork shoulder
- 1 onion, diced
- 1 Tablespoon *(5 g)* fresh ginger, grated
- 2 Tablespoons *(30 ml)* apple cider vinegar
- 1 Tablespoon *(15 g)* salt
- 1 teaspoon *(1 g)* black pepper
- 1 cup *(240 ml)* water

instructions
1. Place all the ingredients into a pressure cooker.
2. Press the Meat/Stew button (normal pressure) and then set the timer for 40 minutes. (The pressure cooker takes a few minutes of prep to get ready and then a few minutes to bring the pressure down, so the total cook time is closer to 1 hour.)

A pressure cooker can make cooking your meats and stews faster - dinner will be ready in no time with them.

the Essential
KETO

PORK AND CASHEW STIR-FRY

Prep Time: 5 minutes | **Cook Time:** 10 minutes | **Total Time:** 15 minutes
Yield: 2 servings
Nutritional Data (estimates) - per serving:
Calories: 440   Fat: 31 g   Net Carbohydrates: 8 g   Protein: 32 g

ingredients
- 1/2 lb *(225 g)* pork tenderloin, sliced thin
- 1 egg, whisked
- 1 bell pepper, diced
- 1 green onion, diced
- 1/3 cup *(40 g)* cashews
- 1 Tablespoon *(5 g)* fresh ginger, grated
- 3 cloves of garlic, minced
- 1 teaspoon *(5 ml)* Chinese chili oil (optional)
- 1 Tablespoon *(15 ml)* sesame oil (optional)
- 2 Tablespoons *(30 ml)* tamari sauce
- Salt to taste
- Avocado oil to cook with

instructions
1. Place the avocado oil into a frying pan and cook the whisked egg. Place it aside on a plate.
2. Add additional avocado oil into the frying pan and cook the pork. Then add in the pepper, onion, and cashews. Saute until the pork is fully cooked, then add back in the cooked egg. Then add in the ginger, garlic, chili oil, sesame oil, tamari sauce, and salt to taste.

You can switch the pork for another meat if you prefer.

SPICY DRY RUB RIBS

Prep Time: 5 minutes | **Cook Time:** 2 hours | **Total Time:** 2 hours 5 minutes
Yield: 2 servings
Nutritional Data (estimates) - per serving:
Calories: 520   Fat: 45 g   Net Carbohydrates: 2 g   Protein: 25 g

INGREDIENTS
- 2 lb *(908 g)* pork spare ribs
- 1 Tablespoon *(15 g)* salt
- 2 Tablespoons *(12 g)* paprika
- 1 Tablespoon *(10 g)* garlic powder
- 1 Tablespoon *(7 g)* onion powder
- 1/2 teaspoon *(1 g)* chili powder or cayenne pepper

INSTRUCTIONS
1. Cut the ribs so that they're in slabs of approx. 4 ribs.
2. Place the ribs in a pot of water (make sure the ribs are submerged in the water) and boil for 1 hour (again, keep the water for broths later). (This is an easy method for cooking tender ribs - there are more complicated methods, but this is the most fool-proof one I've found.)
3. Preheat oven to 325 F *(160 C)*.
4 Mix together the salt, paprika, garlic powder, onion powder, and cayenne pepper to form the rub. Taste the rub to see if you want to add in more of any of the spices.
5. Dip each set of ribs into the rub and place in a baking pan. Place foil over the baking pan and bake for 40 minutes. Remove the foil and bake for another 20 minutes.

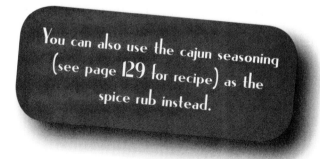

You can also use the cajun seasoning (see page 129 for recipe) as the spice rub instead.

CHINESE PORK SPARE RIBS

Prep Time: 10 minutes | *Cook Time:* 1 hour 20 minutes | *Total Time:* 1 hour 30 minutes
Yield: 4 servings
Nutritional Data (estimates) - per serving:
Calories: 520   Fat: 45 g   Net Carbohydrates: 2 g   Protein: 25 g

ingredients

- 4 lb *(1.8 kg)* pork spare ribs *(or back ribs)*, chopped into individual ribs
- 3 star anise
- 20 Szechuan peppercorns
- 2 Tablespoons *(30 g)* salt *(optional)*
- 3 cloves of garlic, minced
- 1/4-inch *(1.25 cm)* chunk of fresh ginger, grated
- 1/4 cup *(17 g)* scallions *(spring onion, diced), divided into 2 parts*
- 4 Tablespoons *(60 ml)* tamari sauce
- 2 Tablespoons *(30 ml)* coconut oil

instructions

1. Place the ribs in a large stockpot filled with water so that the ribs are covered.
2. After the water starts boiling, skim off any foam that forms on the top of the broth.
3. Add star anise, Szechuan peppercorns, and salt to the pot and simmer until the meat is cooked and soft *(approx. 45 minutes)*.
4. Remove the ribs from the pot but keep the broth (pour it through a sieve to remove all solids). The broth *(by itself)* is wonderful to drink with just a bit of salt, or else you can use it as the base for soups.
5. In a small bowl, mix together the grated ginger, scallions, minced garlic, tamari sauce, and coconut oil.
6. Heat up a skillet *(or wok if you have one)* on high heat and add the ribs in batches to it. Divide the mixture so that you will have enough for each batch of ribs. Coat each batch of ribs on both sides with the mixture. Double the mixture if you prefer more sauce on the ribs.
7. Sauté the ribs on high heat until they brown and no more liquid remains in the skillet.

MU SHU PORK

Prep Time: 15 minutes | **Cook Time:** 15 minutes | **Total Time:** 30 minutes
Yield: 2 servings
Nutritional Data (estimates) - per serving:
Calories: 340   Fat: 18 g   Net Carbohydrates: 7 g   Protein: 35 g

ingredients

- 1/2 lb *(225 g)* pork tenderloin, cut into small thin 1-inch long strips
- 3 eggs, whisked
- 15 Napa cabbage leaves, chopped into thin strips
- 1 cup *(89 g)* shiitake mushrooms, sliced
- 1 8-ounce *(227 g)* can of sliced bamboo shoots or asparagus
- 1/2 teaspoon *(1 g)* fresh ginger, grated
- 1 Tablespoon *(15 ml)* tamari sauce
- 1/2 teaspoon *(2.5 ml)* apple cider vinegar
- Salt to taste
- 1 Tablespoon + 1 teaspoon *(18 ml total)* coconut oil to cook in
- 1/4 cup *(17 g)* scallions *(for garnish)*
- Lettuce leaves to serve pork in *(optional)*

instructions

1. Add 1 Tablespoon *(15 ml)* of coconut oil to a skillet on medium heat.
2. Add a little bit of salt to the whisked eggs and pour the mixture into the skillet. Let it cook undisturbed into a pancake. Flip the egg pancake once it's cooked most of the way through *(it needs to be fairly solid when you flip it)*. Cook for a few more minutes, then place on a cutting board and cut into thin 1-inch long strips.
3. Cook the pork in a teaspoon of coconut oil. Stir with a spatula to make sure the strips don't clump together.
4. Once the pork is cooked, add in the strips of eggs, sliced mushrooms, sliced Napa cabbage, and bamboo shoots. Add in the ginger, tamari sauce, and apple cider vinegar.
5. Cook until the cabbage and mushrooms are soft. Then add salt to taste.
6. Sprinkle the scallions on top for garnish and serve dish in lettuce cups or by itself.

PAN-FRIED PORK TENDERLOIN

Prep Time: 5 minutes | *Cook Time:* 25 minutes | *Total Time:* 30 minutes
Yield: 2 servings
Nutritional Data (estimates) - per serving:
Calories: 330   Fat: 15 g   Net Carbohydrates: 0 g   Protein: 47 g

ingredients
- 1 lb *(454 g)* pork tenderloin
- Salt and pepper to taste
- 1 Tablespoon *(15 ml)* coconut oil to cook in

instructions
1. Cut the 1 lb pork tenderloin in half (to create 2 equal shorter halves).
2. Place the 1 Tablespoon of coconut oil into a frying pan on a medium heat.
3. Place the 2 pork tenderloin pieces into the pan.
4. Leave the pork to cook on its side. Sprinkle salt and pepper to taste. Once that side is cooked, turn using tongs to cook the other sides. Keep turning and cooking until the pork looks cooked on all sides.
5. Cook all sides of the pork until the meat thermometer shows an internal temperature of just below 145 F (63 C). The pork will keep on cooking a bit after you take it out of the pan.
6. Let the pork sit for a few minutes and then slice into 1-inch thick slices with a sharp knife.

The pork will be slightly pink on the inside, but if the internal temperature reaches 145 F, then it will be safe to eat (under the new USDA guidelines). The pork will also be tender and delicious!

the Essential
KETO

Fish & Seafood Entrees

CHAPTER 3D

BREADED COD WITH GARLIC GHEE SAUCE

Prep Time: 10 minutes | **Cook Time:** 20 minutes | **Total Time:** 30 minutes
Yield: 4 servings
Nutritional Data (estimates) - per serving:
Calories: 280   Fat: 15 g   Net Carbohydrates: 5 g   Protein: 25 g

ingredients

- 4 cod filets *(approx. 0.3 lb or 136 g each)*
- 1/2 cup *(30 g)* coconut flour (or almond flour)
- 2 Tablespoons *(15 g)* coconut flakes
- 3 Tablespoons *(30 g)* garlic powder
- 1 Tablespoon *(7 g)* onion powder
- 1 egg, whisked
- Salt to taste
- 2 Tablespoons *(30 ml)* ghee
- 3 cloves of garlic, minced
- Coconut oil for greasing baking tray

instructions

1. Preheat oven to 425 F (220 C).
2. In a large bowl, whisk an egg.
3. In a separate large bowl, combine the breading ingredients (coconut flour, coconut flakes, garlic powder, and onion powder). Add in salt and taste the mixture to see how much salt you like.
4. Cover a baking tray with aluminum foil and grease with coconut oil.
5. Dip each cod filet first into the whisked egg and then into the breading mixture and cover it well with the breading. Place the breaded cod onto the baking tray.
6. Bake for 15-20 minutes until the cod flakes easily.
7. While the cod is in the oven, prepare the garlic ghee sauce by melting the ghee slightly and adding in the minced garlic.
8. Pour the garlic ghee sauce on top of the breaded cod and serve.

FISH TACOS

Prep Time: 30 minutes | **Cook Time:** 15 minutes | **Total Time:** 45 minutes
Yield: 2 servings
Nutritional Data (estimates) - per serving:
Calories: 400   Fat: 15 g   Net Carbohydrates: 9 g   Protein: 50 g

ingredients
For the fish:
- 1 lb *(454 g)* tilapia *(halibut/cod)*, cut into 1/2 inch by 3/4 inch *(1 cm by 2 cm)* strips
- 1/2 cup *(56 g)* coconut flour
- 1 Tablespoon *(10 g)* garlic powder
- 2 teaspoons *(10 g)* salt
- 2 teaspoons *(5 g)* cumin powder
- Coconut oil for frying

For the white sauce:
- 1/2 cup *(120 g)* mayo (see page 125)
- 1 Tablespoon *(15 ml)* lime juice
- 1 teaspoon *(2 g)* dried oregano
- 1/2 teaspoon *(1 g)* cumin powder
- Dash of chili powder

To eat:
- 4-6 lettuce leaves
- 1/4 cup *(60 g)* salsa *(optional)*
- 2 Tablespoons *(4 g)* cilantro, chopped
- 4-6 lime wedges

instructions
1. To make the white sauce, mix all the sauce ingredients together with a fork.
2. Mix together the coconut flour, garlic powder, cumin powder, and salt in a bowl.
3. Drop the fish strips into the bowl and coat with the coconut flour mixture.
4. Heat up coconut oil in a saucepan on high heat (the coconut oil should be approx. 1/2 inch (1-2 cm) deep).
5. Carefully add the coated fish strips to the hot coconut oil.
6. Fry until the coconut flour coating turns a golden brown color *(approx. 5 minutes)*.
7. Place fried fish strips in a bowl lined with a paper towel to soak up excess oil.
8. To eat, place fish strips on a lettuce leaf with salsa, cilantro, and white sauce. Serve with lime wedges.

The Essential
KETO

POPCORN SHRIMP

Prep Time: 5 minutes | **Cook Time:** 20 minutes | **Total Time:** 25 minutes
Yield: 2 servings
Nutritional Data (estimates) - per serving:
Calories: 390   Fat: 23 g   Net Carbohydrates: 3 g   Protein: 30 g

ingredients
- 1/2 lb *(225 g)* small shrimp, peeled
- 2 eggs, whisked
- 6 Tablespoons *(36 g)* cajun seasoning (see page 129 for recipe)
- 6 Tablespoons *(42 g)* coconut flour
- Coconut oil for frying

instructions
1. Melt the coconut oil in a saucepan (use enough coconut oil so that it's 1/2 inch *(1-2 cm)* deep) or deep fryer.
2. Place the whisked eggs into a large bowl, and in another large bowl, combine the coconut flour and seasoning.
3. Drop a handful of the shrimp into the whisked eggs and stir around so that each shrimp is coated.
4. Then take the shrimp out of the whisked eggs and place into the seasoning bowl. Coat the shrimp with the coconut flour and seasoning mixture.
5. Place the coated shrimp into the hot oil and fry until golden. Try not to stir the pot and don't place too many shrimp into the pot at once *(make sure all the shrimp is touching the oil)*.
6. Using a slotted spoon, remove the shrimp and place on paper towels to absorb the excess oil. Repeat for the rest of the shrimp (change the oil if there are too many solids in it).
7. Cool for 10 minutes *(the outside will get crisp)*.

ROSEMARY BAKED SALMON

Prep Time: 5 minutes | **Cook Time:** 30 minutes | **Total Time**: 35 minutes
Yield: 2 servings
Nutritional Data (estimates) - per serving:
Calories: 430   Fat: 18 g   Net Carbohydrates: 0 g   Protein: 63 g

ingredients
- 2 salmon filets *(fresh or defrosted)*
- 1 Tablespoon *(2 g)* fresh rosemary leaves
- 1/4 cup *(60 ml)* olive oil
- 1 teaspoon *(5 g)* salt *(optional or to taste)*

instructions
1. Preheat oven to 350 F *(175 C)*.
2. Mix the olive oil, rosemary, and salt together in a bowl.
3. Place one salmon filet at a time into the mixture and rub mixture onto the filet.
4. Wrap each filet in a piece of aluminum foil with some of the remaining mixture.
5. Bake for 25-30 minutes.

EASY SALMON STEW

Prep Time: 10 minutes | **Cook Time:** 20 minutes | **Total Time:** 30 minutes
Yield: 2 servings
Nutritional Data (estimates) - per serving:
Calories: 450   Fat: 12 g   Net Carbohydrates: 7 g   Protein: 70 g

ingredients
- 4 cups *(1 l)* chicken broth (or bone broth)
- 2 salmon filets *(1/2 lb or 225 g)*, diced
- 2 zucchinis, diced
- 4 button mushrooms, diced
- 2 cups *(200 g)* chopped celery
- 1/2 cup *(16 g)* chopped cilantro
- Salt and pepper (to taste)

instructions
1. Place all the vegetables with the broth into a pot and simmer for 15 minutes.
2. Add the diced salmon and simmer for another 5 minutes. Add salt and pepper.

CUCUMBER GINGER SHRIMP

Prep Time: 5 minutes | **Cook Time:** 10 minutes | **Total Time:** 15 minutes
Yield: 1 serving
Nutritional Data (estimates) - per serving:
Calories: 250   Fat: 16 g   Net Carbohydrates: 4 g   Protein: 20 g

ingredients
- 1 large cucumber, peeled and sliced into 1/2-inch round slices
- 10-15 large shrimp/prawns (defrosted if frozen)
- 1 teaspoon *(1 g)* fresh ginger, grated
- Salt to taste
- Coconut oil to cook with

instructions
1. Place 1 Tablespoon (*15 ml*) of coconut oil into a frying pan on medium heat.
2. Add in the ginger and the cucumber and sauté for 2-3 minutes.
3. Add in the shrimp and cook until they turn pink and are no longer translucent.
4. Add salt to taste and serve.

AVOCADO TUNA BOWL WITH TAHINI TAMARI PASTE

Prep Time: 10 minutes | **Cook Time:** 0 minutes | **Total Time:** 10 minutes
Yield: 2 servings
Nutritional Data (estimates) - per serving:
Calories: 667   Fat: 48 g   Net Carbohydrates: 7 g   Protein: 46 g

ingredients
- 1 large avocado, destoned and diced
- 2 Tablespoons *(30 ml)* lime juice
- 2 Tablespoons *(30 ml)* olive oil, to cook with
- 2 cans of tuna *(340 g or 12 oz)*, drained and flaked
- 2 Tablespoons of fresh cilantro, finely chopped
- 2 Tablespoons *(30 ml)* tahini sauce
- 3 Tablespoons *(45 ml)* gluten-free tamari sauce or coconut aminos
- 1 Tablespoon *(15 ml)* sesame oil

instructions
1. To make the tahini tamari paste, mix together the tahini, tamari sauce, and sesame oil.
2. To make the tuna salad, mix the lime juice, cilantro, olive oil, and tuna together.
3. To serve, place the diced avocado into a bowl, then top with the tuna and paste.

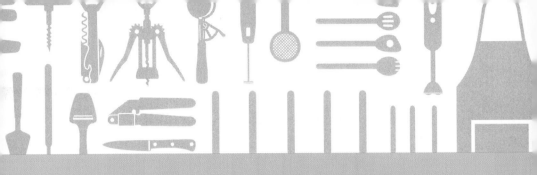

Other Entrees

CHAPTER 3E

SLOW COOKER OXTAIL STEW

Prep Time: 10 minutes | **Cook Time:** 8 hours | **Total Time:** 8 hours 10 minutes
Yield: 4 servings
Nutritional Data (estimates) - per serving:
Calories: 380   Fat: 20 g   Net Carbohydrates: 4 g   Protein: 40 g

ingredients

- 2 lb *(908 g)* beef oxtail
- 1 large onion, chopped
- 1 zucchini, chopped
- 1 carrot, chopped
- 2 cups *(480 ml)* chicken broth
- 1 Tablespoon *(5 g)* fresh ginger, chopped
- 5 cloves of garlic, peeled but whole
- Salt to taste

instructions

1. Place the oxtail, chopped onion, carrot, zucchini, chicken broth, ginger, garlic, and salt into the slow cooker. Cook for 8 hours until the meat is tender.

TURKEY ARUGULA SALAD

Prep Time: 5 minutes | **Cook Time:** 0 minutes | **Total Time**: 5 minutes
Yield: 2 servings
Nutritional Data (estimates) - per serving:
Calories: 260   Fat: 15 g   Net Carbohydrates: 6 g   Protein: 20 g

ingredients

- 3.5 oz *(100 g)* arugula leaves
- 4 oz *(115 g)* turkey deli meat or turkey breast meat, diced
- 10 raspberries (or blueberries)
- 1 cucumber, peeled and diced
- 2 Tablespoons *(30 ml)* olive oil
- Juice from 1/2 a lime

instructions

1. Toss all the ingredients together in a large bowl and enjoy.

CUMIN CRUSTED LAMB CHOPS

Prep Time: 15 minutes | **Cook Time:** 15 minutes | **Total Time:** 30 minutes
Yield: 4 servings
Nutritional Data (estimates) - per serving:
Calories: 700   Fat: 60 g   Net Carbohydrates: 2 g   Protein: 45 g

ingredients

- 2 racks of lamb *(3 lb or 1.3 kg)*
- ¾ cup *(72 g)* cumin powder
- 3 Tablespoons *(18 g)* paprika
- 1 teaspoon *(1 g)* chili powder (more if preferred)
- 1 Tablespoon *(15 g)* salt (less if preferred)

instructions

1. Cut the racks of lamb into individual lamb chops (approx 20 chops).
2. Combine the spices and salt and dip the lamb chops into it.
3. Grill the lamb until done to the level you enjoy.

LAMB AND MINT MEATBALLS

Prep Time: 15 minutes | **Cook Time**: 15 minutes | **Total Time:** 30 minutes
Yield: 4 servings
Nutritional Data (estimates) - per serving:
Calories: 370   Fat: 30 g   Net Carbohydrates: 1 g   Protein: 20 g

ingredients

- 1 lb *(454 g)* lamb meat
- 1 egg
- 1/2 large onion
- 1/2 teaspoon *(1 g)* cumin powder
- 10 fresh mint leaves
- 1 teaspoon *(5 g)* salt
- Avocado oil to cook in

instructions

1. Place all the ingredients (except the oil) into the food processor and process well. Form small golf-ball sized meatballs (approx. 25) from the mixture.
2. Place avocado oil into a frying pan and fry the meatballs in batches.

LIVER AND ONIONS

Prep Time: 10 minutes | **Cook Time:** 20 minutes | **Total Time:** 30 minutes
Yield: 2 servings
Nutritional Data (estimates) - per serving:
Calories: 460   Fat: 24 g   Net Carbohydrates: 8 g   Protein: 45 g

ingredients

- 1 lb (*454 g*) liver, diced
- 1 large onion, diced
- 2 Tablespoons (*30 ml*) ghee (or coconut oil)
- 2 slices bacon
- Salt and pepper to taste

instructions

1. Cook the bacon in a pan and then break into small bits.
2. Place the ghee into a frying pan. Add the diced onion and cook until translucent.
3. Then add in the diced liver and saute until cooked. Add in the bacon bits and salt and pepper to taste.

Make this delicious traditional liver and onions dish to get more liver into your diet - it's super nutritious.

Side Dishes

CHAPTER 4

CAULIFLOWER WHITE "RICE"

Prep Time: 10 minutes | ***Cook Time:*** 15 minutes | ***Total Time:*** 25 minutes
Yield: 2 servings
Nutritional Data (estimates) - per serving:
Calories: 90   Fat: 7 g   Net Carbohydrates: 4 g   Protein: 3 g

ingredients
- 1/2 head *(approx. 220 g)* of cauliflower, chopped into small florets
- 1 Tablespoon *(15 ml)* coconut oil

instructions
1. Process the cauliflower in the food processor until it forms very small "rice"-like pieces. Squeeze out excess water.
2. Add 1 Tablespoon of coconut oil into a large pot. Add in the cauliflower and let it cook on a medium heat. Stir regularly to make sure it doesn't burn. Cook until tender but not mushy.

GARLIC ZUCCHINI SAUTE

Prep Time: 5 minutes | ***Cook Time:*** 12 minutes | ***Total Time:*** 17 minutes
Yield: 4 servings
Nutritional Data (estimates) - per serving:
Calories: 70   Fat: 4 g   Net Carbohydrates: 4 g   Protein: 0 g

ingredients
- 2 lb *(908 g)* zucchini, chopped into small pieces or slices
- 6 cloves of garlic, minced
- Olive oil to saute in

instructions
1. Add olive oil into a skillet on medium heat. Add in the zucchini and saute until they're softened (approx. 10 minutes). Add the garlic and saute for 1-2 minutes more.

MICROWAVE QUICK BREAD

Prep Time: 3.5 minutes | **Cook Time:** 1.5 minutes | **Total Time:** 5 minutes
Yield: 2 servings
Nutritional Data (estimates) - per serving:
Calories: 260   Fat: 26 g   Net Carbohydrates: 2 g   Protein: 6 g

ingredients

- 1/3 cup *(35 g)* almond flour
- 1/2 teaspoon *(2 g)* baking powder
- 1 egg, whisked
- 2.5 Tablespoons *(37 ml)* ghee or coconut oil, melted

instructions

1. Grease a mug and mix all the ingredients in it with a fork.
2. Microwave for 90 seconds on high. *(You may need to adjust the time for your microwave settings.)*
3. Cool for a few minutes, pop out of mug gently and slice into 4 thin slices.

Don't want to use a microwave? No worries : check out the ovenbaked loaf of bread on page 115 instead

the Essential
KETO

CREAMY CAULIFLOWER MASH

Prep Time: 10 minutes | *Cook Time:* 10 minutes | *Total Time:* 20 minutes
Yield: 2 servings
Nutritional Data (estimates) - per serving:
Calories: 200   Fat: 20 g   Net Carbohydrates: 4 g   Protein: 4 g

ingredients
- 1/2 head of cauliflower *(approx. 220 g)*, broken into small florets
- 2 Tablespoons *(30 ml)* ghee (or coconut oil)
- 1/4 cup *(60 ml)* coconut milk, from a can shaken & at room temp
- Salt to taste

instructions
1. Place the cauliflower florets into a large microwaveable bowl with 1/4 cup of water at the bottom. Microwave on high until they are softened (around 10-12 minutes). Check every 3 minutes to make sure there's water in the bowl still. Alternatively, you can steam the cauliflower florets in a steamer.
2. Blend the cauliflower with ghee, coconut milk, and salt until smooth.

SPINACH ALMOND SAUTE

Prep Time: 0 minutes | *Cook Time:* 10 minutes | *Total Time:* 10 minutes
Yield: 2 servings
Nutritional Data (estimates) - per serving:
Calories: 150   Fat: 11 g   Net Carbohydrates: 4 g   Protein: 8 g

ingredients
- 1 lb *(454 g)* spinach leaves
- 3 Tablespoons *(12 g)* almond slices
- Salt to taste
- 1 Tablespoon *(15 ml)* avocado oil for cooking

instructions
1. Place the 1 Tablespoon of avocado oil into a large pot on medium heat.
2. Add in the spinach and let it cook down.
3. Once the spinach is cooked down, add the salt to taste and stir.
4. Before serving, stir in the almond slices.

EASY BACON BRUSSELS SPROUTS

Prep Time: 5 minutes | *Cook Time:* 20 minutes | *Total Time:* 25 minutes
Yield: 6 servings
Nutritional Data (estimates) - per serving:
Calories: 400   Fat: 35 g   Net Carbohydrates: 6 g   Protein: 14 g

ingredients
- 2 lbs *(908 g)* Brussels sprouts
- 1 lb *(454 g)* bacon, uncooked

instructions
1. Boil the Brussels sprouts for 10 minutes until tender.
2. While the Brussels sprouts are boiling, chop the bacon into small pieces *(approx. 1/2-inch wide)*, and cook the bacon pieces in a large pot on medium heat. When the bacon is crispy, add in the drained Brussels sprouts.
3. Cook for 10 more minutes on high heat, stirring occasionally to make sure nothing gets burnt on the bottom of the pan.

TURMERIC CAULIFLOWER PANCAKES

Prep Time: 10 minutes | **Cook Time:** 40 minutes | **Total Time:** 50 minutes
Yield: 8 servings
Nutritional Data (estimates) - per serving:
Calories: 123   Fat: 9 g   Net Carbohydrates: 3 g   Protein: 5 g

ingredients
- 1 head of cauliflower, broken into florets
- 2 eggs, whisked
- 1 cup *(120 g)* almond flour
- 2 Tablespoons *(12 g)* turmeric powder
- 2 cloves of garlic, peeled and minced
- 1 Tablespoon *(15 ml)* coconut oil, for greasing the baking tray
- Salt and pepper, to taste

instructions
1. Preheat oven to 350 F *(175 C)*.
2. Steam the cauliflower florets until softened.
3. Mash the cauliflower and mix with the eggs, almond flour, turmeric, and garlic. Season with salt and pepper.
4. Form 8 flat patties. Place on a greased baking tray and bake for 30 minutes until slightly browned.

TANGY RED CABBAGE COLESLAW

Prep Time: 10 minutes | **Cook Time:** 0 minutes | **Total Time:** 10 minutes
Yield: 4 servings
Nutritional Data (estimates) - per serving:
Calories: 164   Fat: 17 g   Net Carbohydrates: 3 g   Protein: 2 g

ingredients
- 2 cups of shredded red cabbage *(approx 1/4 head of cabbage)*
- 1/4 red onion, sliced
- 1/4 cup *(20 g)* walnuts, chopped
- 2 Tablespoons *(30 ml)* lemon juice
- 1/4 cup *(60 ml)* mayo (see page 125 for recipe)
- 1 teaspoon *(5 ml)* mustard

instructions
1. Toss all the ingredients together well and enjoy.

CAULIFLOWER NOTATO SALAD

Prep Time: 5 minutes | **Cook Time:** 10 minutes | **Total Time:** 15 minutes
Yield: 4 servings
Nutritional Data (estimates) - per serving:
Calories: 136   Fat: 12 g   Net Carbohydrates: 4 g   Protein: 3 g

ingredients
- 1 head of cauliflower, broken into florets
- 2 Tablespoons of chives, finely diced
- 1/4 cup *(60 ml)* mayo (see page 125 for recipe)
- 2 teaspoons *(10 ml)* mustard
- Salt and pepper to taste

instructions
1. Boil or steam the cauliflower florets until tender. Run immediately under cold water to cool. Then drain well.
2. Toss the florets with the chives, mayo, mustard, and salt and pepper.

ROASTED CAULIFLOWER

Prep Time: 15 minutes | *Cook Time:* 1 hour 15 minutes
Total Time: 1 hour 30 minutes | *Yield:* 4 servings
Nutritional Data (estimates) - per serving:
Calories: 90   Fat: 7 g   Net Carbohydrates: 3 g   Protein: 0 g

ingredients
- Half of a large cauliflower *(approx. 220 g)*, broken into florets
- 2 teaspoons *(4 g)* turmeric powder or garlic powder or Italian seasoning
- 2 teaspoons *(10 g)* salt
- 2 Tablespoons *(30 ml)* olive oil

instructions
1. Preheat oven to 350 F *(175 C)*.
2. Mix the cauliflower florets with the spice/herb, salt, and olive oil.
3. Spread the florets out in a baking tray and bake covered with foil for 75 minutes.

SUPER FAST AVOCADO SALAD

Prep Time: 5 minutes | *Cook Time:* 0 minutes | *Total Time:* 5 minutes
Yield: 2 servings
Nutritional Data (estimates) - per serving:
Calories: 220   Fat: 21 g   Net Carbohydrates: 2 g   Protein: 2 g

ingredients
- 1 ripe avocado
- 1 Tablespoon *(15 ml)* olive oil
- 1/2 Tablespoon *(7 ml)* lemon juice
- Salt to taste

instructions
1. Cut a ripe avocado in half.
2. Remove the pit, and using a small knife carefully score each half into cubes. Then use a spoon to scoop out the avocado cubes.
3. Toss the avocado cubes with olive oil, lemon juice, and salt.

Desserts, Breads, & Snacks

CHAPTER 5

RED VELVET COOKIES

Prep Time: 15 minutes | **Cook Time:** 15 minutes | **Total Time:** 30 minutes
Yield: 8 servings
Nutritional Data (estimates) - per serving:
Calories: 227   Fat: 25 g   Net Carbohydrates: 3 g   Protein: 7 g

ingredients

- 2 cups *(240 g)* almond flour
- 2 Tablespoons *(14 g)* flaxmeal
- 1/4 cup *(28 g)* coconut flour
- 3 Tablespoons *(18 g)* unsweetened cacao powder
- 1 beet, raw, peeled and diced
- 2 Tablespoons *(30 ml)* apple cider vinegar
- 1/3 cup *(80 ml)* ghee
- 1/3-1/2 cup erythritol
(or Keto sweetener, to taste)
- 1 egg, whisked
- 1/2 teaspoon *(1 g)* baking soda
- 1 teaspoon *(5 ml)* vanilla extract
- Dash of salt

instructions

1. Preheat oven to 350 F *(175 C)*.
2. Puree the beet and add in the vinegar and ghee.
3. Mix all the cookie ingredients together in a bowl until a soft dough forms.
4. Form small balls from the dough (use a Tablespoon scoop). Press into a round cookie and place onto a parchment paper lined baking tray. The cookies will spread so make sure to leave enough room between the cookies. Makes around 24 small cookies.
5. Bake for 12-15 minutes. Let cool before enjoying.

CHOCOLATE COFFEE COCONUT TRUFFLES

Prep Time: 10 minutes | **Cook Time:** 5 hours set time
Total Time: 10 minutes + 5 hours | **Yield:** 6 servings
Nutritional Data (estimates) - per serving:
Calories: 160   Fat: 15 g   Net Carbohydrates: 3 g   Protein: 2 g

ingredients

- 1/2 cup *(120 g)* coconut butter (see page 130 for recipe), melted
- 3 Tablespoons *(15 g)* 100% cacao powder
- 1 Tablespoon *(5 g)* ground coffee beans
- 1 Tablespoon *(5 g)* unsweetened coconut flakes
- Dash of stevia (optional)
- 1 Tablespoon *(15 ml)* coconut oil, melted

instructions

1. Mix all the ingredients together and pour into an ice-cube tray or muffin cups.
2. Freeze for 4-5 hours. Defrost at room temperature for 15-20 minutes before serving.

CHOCOLATE CHIA PUDDING

Prep Time: 5 minutes | **Cook Time:** 8 hours set time | **Total Time:** 5 minutes + 8 hrs
Yield: 2 servings
Nutritional Data (estimates) - per serving:
Calories: 300   Fat: 24 g   Net Carbohydrates: 3 g   Protein: 8 g

ingredients

- 2 Tablespoons *(10 g)* unsweetened cacao powder
- 1 cup *(240 ml)* unsweetened coconut milk
- 1/3 cup *(215 g)* chia seeds
- 1 Tablespoon *(5 g)* unsweetened shredded coconut (for topping)
- Spices and/or sweetener of choice

instructions

1. Mix together all the ingredients (except the shredded coconut) in a bowl and refrigerate overnight.
2. Blend the mixture until smooth. Pour into cups and top with shredded coconut.

BLACK & WHITE LAYERED PEPPERMINT PATTIES

Prep Time: 15 minutes | *Cook Time:* 3 hours set time
Total Time: 15 minutes + 3 hrs | *Yield:* 12 servings
Nutritional Data (estimates) - per serving:
Calories: 100   Fat: 10 g   Net Carbohydrates: 2 g   Protein: 1 g

ingredients

For the white layers:
- ½ cup *(120 g)* coconut butter
- ¼ cup *(20 g)* unsweetened shredded coconut
- 2 Tablespoons *(30 ml)* coconut oil
- 1 teaspoon *(5 ml)* peppermint extract (add more to taste)
- Erythritol and stevia, to taste (optional)

For the black layers:
- 4 oz *(115 g)* 100% dark chocolate
- 4 Tablespoons *(60 ml)* coconut oil

instructions

1. To make the white layers, soften the coconut butter and the 2 tablespoons of coconut oil and mix them together with the unsweetened shredded coconut, sweetener, and peppermint extract.

2. Spoon 2 teaspoons of the white mixture into each mini muffin cup and refrigerate for 1 hour to set. Check this layer is solid before proceeding to the next step. If you don't have a mini muffin tray, then use a regular muffin tray - serving size will be half of a patty.

3. To make the black layers, melt the 4 tablespoons of coconut oil and the 4 oz dark chocolate and combine together well. Spoon 1 teaspoon of the black mixture into each mini muffin cup so that it forms a thin layer above the already solid white layer. Set in fridge for 1 hour. Check this layer is solid before going to the next step.

4. Repeat steps 2 and 3 for as many layers as you want.

FRESHLY BAKED LOAF OF BREAD

Prep Time: 10 minutes | **Cook Time:** 1 hour| **Total Time:** 1 hour 10 minutes
Yield: 8 servings
Nutritional Data (estimates) - per serving:
Calories: 400   Fat: 41 g   Net Carbohydrates: 5 g   Protein: 11 g

ingredients
- 3 cups *(330g)* almond flour
- 3 Tablespoons *(45 g)* whey protein powder *(optional)*
- 1/2 cup + 2 Tablespoons *(150 ml)* coconut oil
- 1/4 cup *(60 ml)* coconut milk (from can)
- 3 eggs, whisked
- 2 teaspoons *(9 g)* baking powder
- 1 teaspoon *(5 g)* baking soda
- 1 Tablespoon *(3 g)* Italian seasoning
- 1/4 teaspoon *(1 g)* salt

instructions
1. Preheat oven to 300 F *(150 C)*.
2. Grease a loaf pan *(9 in by 5 in (22.5 cm by 12.5 cm))*.
3. Mix together all ingredients and pour batter into the pan evenly.
4. Bake for 60 minutes. Let cool, flip out of the loaf pan, and cut into slices with a bread knife.

You don't have to add whey protein, but it helps to make the bread a lot more fluffy and soft

JALAPEÑO "CORN" BREAD

Prep Time: 10 minutes | **Cook Time:** 20 minutes | **Total Time:** 30 minutes
Yield: 6 servings
Nutritional Data (estimates) - per serving:
Calories: 150   Fat: 15 g   Net Carbohydrates: 2 g   Protein: 5 g

ingredients

- 3/4 cup *(83 g)* almond flour
- 1/4 cup *(28 g)* coconut flour
- 2 teaspoons *(9 g)* baking powder
- 1 teaspoon *(5 g)* salt
- Very small dash of stevia
- 3 eggs
- 1/2 cup *(120 ml)* coconut milk
- 3 jalapeño peppers, diced
- Coconut oil for greasing muffin pan or use muffin liners

instructions

1. Preheat oven to 350 F *(175 C)*.
2. Mix together all the ingredients well and pour the batter into a 12-muffin pan.
3. Bake for 20 minutes.

SAVORY ITALIAN CRACKERS

Prep Time: 15 minutes | **Cook Time:** 10 minutes | **Total Time:** 25 minutes
Yield: 4 servings
Nutritional Data (estimates) - per serving:
Calories: 280   Fat: 25 g   Net Carbohydrates: 3 g   Protein: 9 g

ingredients
- 1.5 cups *(165 g)* almond flour
- 1 egg
- 2 Tablespoons *(30 ml)* olive oil
- 3/4 teaspoon *(4 g)* salt
- 1/4 teaspoon *(0.5 g)* basil
- 1/2 teaspoon *(1 g)* thyme
- 1/4 teaspoon *(0.5 g)* oregano
- 1/2 teaspoon *(1 g)* onion powder
- 1/4 teaspoon *(0.5 g)* garlic powder

instructions
1. Preheat oven to 350 F *(175 C)*.
2. Mix all the ingredients well to form a dough.
3. Shape dough into a long rectangular log (use some foil or cling film to pack the dough tight) and then cut into thin slices *(approximately 0.2 inches (0.5 cm) thick)*. Gently place each slice onto a parchment paper-lined baking tray. It makes approx. 20-30 crackers, depending on size.
4. Bake for 10-12 minutes.

CHOCOLATE CASHEW ICE CREAM

Prep Time: 10 minutes | **Cook Time:** varies, for making cashew cheese and freezing
ice cream
Total Time: varies | **Yield:** 6 servings
Nutritional Data (estimates) - per serving:
Calories: 131   Fat: 11 g   Net Carbohydrates: 3 g   Protein: 3 g

ingredients
- 1 cup *(240 ml)* cashew cheese (see page 127 for recipe)
- 1/4 cup *(60 ml)* coconut cream
- 1 oz *(28 g)* 100% dark chocolate, melted
- Erythritol and stevia, to taste

instructions
1. Blend all the ingredients together really well.
2. Pour into a container and freeze.
3. Best enjoyed after 1-2 hours. If you freeze it for longer, then you'll need to defrost it first to soften it before enjoying.

CHOCOLATE COVERED PECANS

Prep Time: 5 min | **Cook Time:** 25 min + 2 hrs set time | **Total Time:** 30 min + 2 hrs
Yield: 4 servings
Nutritional Data (estimates) - per serving:
Calories: 160   Fat: 15 g   Net Carbohydrates: 5 g   Protein: 3 g

ingredients
- 40-45 pecan halves *(approx. 2.5 oz)*
- 2 oz *(56 g)* 100% dark chocolate
- Spices of your choosing - my favorites were cinnamon, nutmeg, and salt

instructions
1. Preheat oven to 350 F *(175 C)*.
2. Place the pecan halves in a single layer on parchment paper. Bake for 7 minutes.
3. Let them cool. Meanwhile, melt the dark chocolate.
4. Dip each pecan half in the melted chocolate with a fork and place back on the parchment paper. Sprinkle spice on top. Refrigerate for 1-2 hours to set.

CARROT CUPCAKES WITH CASHEW CHEESE FROSTING

Prep Time: 15 minutes | **Cook Time:** 30 minutes | **Total Time:** 45 minutes
Yield: 16 servings
Nutritional Data (estimates) - per serving:
Calories: 210   Fat: 21 g   Net Carbohydrates: 2 g   Protein: 4 g

ingredients

For the cupcakes:
- 3 eggs, whisked
- 1/2 cup erythritol (or to taste)
- 2 carrots *(150 g)*, shredded (squeeze out as much of the liquid as possible)
- 2 teaspoons *(10 ml)* vanilla extract
- 1 cup *(120 g)* almond flour
- 2 Tablespoons *(14 g)* flaxmeal
- 1/4 cup *(20 g)* shredded coconut
- 1/2 cup *(59 g)* walnuts, chopped
- 3/4 cup *(180 ml)* ghee or coconut oil
- 2 teaspoons *(9 g)* baking powder
- 1/2 teaspoon *(2 g)* baking soda
- 2 teaspoons *(4 g)* cinnamon powder
- 1 teaspoon *(2 g)* ginger powder
- 1 Tablespoon *(15 ml)* apple cider vinegar

- Dash of nutmeg
- Dash of salt

For the frosting:
- 1/4 cup *(60 ml)* cashew cheese (see page 127 for recipe)
- 2 Tablespoons *(30 ml)* coconut cream
- 2 Tablespoons *(30 ml)* coconut oil
- Erythritol or stevia, to taste
- 1/2 teaspoon *(3 ml)* vanilla extract
- Dash of salt

For the topping:
- Small handful of chopped walnuts and shredded carrot

instructions

1. Preheat oven to 350 F *(175 C)*.
2. Mix all the cupcake ingredients together.
3. Pour into a cupcake pan (makes approx. 12 cupcakes) and bake for 30 minutes.
4. Meanwhile make the frosting by blending all the ingredients together (don't melt any of the ingredients - just keep them at room temperature and blend them and if it gets too liquidy, then refrigerate them for a bit to let it solidify more). Spread on top of the cupcakes once they're cooled. Top with leftover chopped walnuts and shredded carrots.

GINGER SPICE COOKIES

Prep Time: 10 minutes | **Cook Time:** 15 minutes | **Total Time:** 25 minutes
Yield: 12 servings
Nutritional Data (estimates) - per serving:
Calories: 200   Fat: 18 g   Net Carbohydrates: 3 g   Protein: 6 g

ingredients

- 2 cups *(280 g)* whole almonds
- 2 Tablespoons *(80 g)* chia seeds
- 1/4 cup *(60 ml)* coconut oil
- 1 egg, whisked
- 3 Tablespoons *(15 g)* fresh ginger, grated
- 2 Tablespoons *(14 g)* cinnamon powder
- 1/2 teaspoon *(1 g)* nutmeg
- 1 teaspoon *(5 g)* baking powder
- Erythritol and stevia, to taste
- Dash of salt

instructions

1. Preheat oven to 350 F *(175 C)*.
2. Food process or blend the whole almonds with the chia seeds.
3. Mix all the ingredients together and form 12 small cookies. Bake for 15 minutes.

Condiments, Seasoning, & Sauces

CHAPTER 6

COCONUT MAYONNAISE

Prep Time: 15 minutes | **Cook Time:** 0 minutes | **Total Time:** 15 minutes
Yield: approx. 1.5 cups
Nutritional Data (estimates) - per tablespoon:
Calories: 80   Fat: 9 g   Net Carbohydrates: 0 g   Protein: 0 g

ingredients
- 2 egg yolks
- 2 Tablespoons *(30 ml)* of apple cider vinegar
- 1 cup *(240 ml)* coconut oil, melted *(but not too hot)*

instructions
1. Blend or whisk the 2 egg yolks with the 2 Tablespoons *(30 ml)* of apple cider vinegar.
2. Slowly add in the coconut oil while blending *(I used a blender and added in the coconut oil from the hole at top of the blender approximately 1/2 tablespoon at a time until it forms a mayo texture).*
3. Add in rest of the oil (and a bit more if you want a less thick texture) and blend well.
4. Use immediately *(if you want to store it in the fridge, then use 1/2 cup olive oil or avocado oil and 1/2 cup coconut oil instead of only coconut oil, as the coconut oil will make the mayo solidify in the fridge. We try to use it within a week.)*

substitutions
- Olive oil or avocado oil can be used instead of coconut oil.
- Spices and herbs can be added for different types of mayo.
- Lemon juice can be used instead of apple cider vinegar (but it gives a different taste to the mayo).

the Essential
KETO
COOKBOOK

CASHEW CHEESE

Prep Time: 10 minutes | ***Cook Time:*** 0 minutes | ***Total Time:*** 10 minutes
Yield: 1 cup
Nutritional Data (estimates) - per tablespoon:
Calories: 32   Fat: 3 g   Net Carbohydrates: 1 g   Protein: 1 g

ingredients
- 1/2 cup *(70 g)* raw cashews, soaked overnight
- 1 Tablespoon *(15 ml)* coconut oil
- 1/2 cup *(120 ml)* water

instructions
1. Place the raw cashews into a bowl of room temperature water so that it covers the cashews, drape a paper towel or tea towel over the bowl to prevent dust settling, and soak overnight.
2. Blend the soaked cashews, 1/2 cup fresh water, and coconut oil until smooth.

Cashew cheese is great as a spread on keto bread, eaten by itself, or spread on cupcakes to create cream cheese frosting

CAESAR DRESSING

Prep Time: 15 minutes | *Cook Time:* 0 minutes | *Total Time:* 15 minutes
Yield: approx. 1.5 cups
Nutritional Data (estimates) - per tablespoon:
Calories: 80   Fat: 9 g   Net Carbohydrates: 0 g   Protein: 0 g

ingredients
- 2 egg yolks
- 1/4 cup *(60 ml)* apple cider vinegar
- 1 cup *(240 ml)* coconut oil, melted
- 6 anchovies
- 2 teaspoons *(9 g)* Dijon mustard
- 2 large cloves of garlic, minced
- 1/4 teaspoon *(1 g)* salt
- 1/4 teaspoon *(1 g)* freshly ground black pepper

instructions
1. Blend or whisk the 2 egg yolks with the apple cider vinegar.
2. Slowly add in the coconut oil while blending until it forms a mayo texture.
3. Add in rest of the oil, the anchovies, mustard, garlic, salt, and pepper and blend well.

COCONUT RANCH DRESSING

Prep Time: 10 minutes | *Cook Time:* 0 minutes | *Total Time:* 10 minutes
Yield: approx. 1/2 cup
Nutritional Data (estimates) - per tablespoon:
Calories: 50   Fat: 6 g   Net Carbohydrates: 0 g   Protein: 0 g

ingredients
- 1/4 cup *(60 ml)* of mayo (see page 125 for recipe)
- 1/4 cup *(60 ml)* coconut milk
- 1 clove of garlic, minced
- 1/2 teaspoon *(1 g)* onion powder
- 1 Tablespoon *(4 g)* fresh parsley, finely chopped *(or 1 tsp (0.5 g) dried parsley)*
- 1 Tablespoon *(3 g)* fresh chives, finely chopped *(or omit)*
- 1 teaspoon *(1 g)* fresh dill, finely chopped *(or 1/2 tsp (0.5 g) dried dill)*
- Dash of salt
- Dash of pepper

instructions
1. Mix together the mayo, coconut milk, onion powder, salt, and pepper with a fork.
2. Gently mix in the garlic and fresh herbs.

HOMEMADE ITALIAN SEASONING

Prep Time: 5 minutes | ***Cook Time:*** 0 minutes | ***Total Time:*** 5 minutes
Yield: 1 cup
Nutritional Data (estimates) - per tablespoon:
Calories: 10   Fat: 0 g   Net Carbohydrates: 1 g   Protein: 0 g

ingredients
- 1/4 cup *(12 g)* dried basil
- 1/4 cup *(12 g)* dried rosemary
- 1/4 cup *(12 g)* dried thyme
- 1/4 cup *(12 g)* dried oregano
- 1 Tablespoon *(10 g)* garlic powder
- 1 Tablespoon *(7 g)* onion powder

instructions
1. Mix all the ingredients together well and store in an airtight container.

CAJUN SEASONING

Prep Time: 5 minutes | ***Cook Time:*** 0 minutes | ***Total Time:*** 5 minutes
Yield: 6 Tablespoons
Nutritional Data (estimates) - per tablespoon:
Calories: 15   Fat: 0 g   Net Carbohydrates: 2 g   Protein: 0 g

ingredients
- 1.5 Tablespoons *(10 g)* paprika
- 1.5 Tablespoons *(15 g)* garlic powder
- 1/2 Tablespoon *(3 g)* onion powder
- 1/2 Tablespoon *(2 g)* black pepper
- 1 teaspoon *(2 g)* cayenne pepper
- 1 teaspoon *(2 g)* dried oregano
- 1 teaspoon *(1 g)* dried thyme
- 1 teaspoon *(1 g)* dried basil
- 1-2 teaspoons *(5-10 g)* of salt *(to taste)*

instructions
1. Mix all the dried spices and herbs together and store in an airtight jar.

the Essential
KETO

SLOW COOKER GHEE

Prep Time: 0 minutes | **Cook Time:** 3 hours | **Total Time:** 3 hours
Yield: 2 cups
Nutritional Data (estimates) - per tablespoon:
Calories: 120   Fat: 14 g   Net Carbohydrates: 0 g   Protein: 0 g

ingredients
• 16 oz *(454 g)* butter

instructions
1. Place butter into slow cooker and place lid on (slightly ajar so that steam escapes).
2. Turn slow cooker on low for 2-3 hours until milk solids brown and fall to bottom.
3. Strain through a cheesecloth into glass jars to store.

Ghee - also known as clarified butter - contains very little casein, lactose or other milk solids, making it less inflammatory

COCONUT BUTTER

Prep Time: 10 minutes | **Cook Time:** 0 minutes | **Total Time:** 10 minutes
Yield: approx. 3 cups
Nutritional Data (estimates) - per tablespoon:
Calories: 60   Fat: 6 g   Net Carbohydrates: 1 g   Protein: 1 g

ingredients
• 6 cups *(480 g)* of unsweetened shredded coconut (or coconut flakes or coconut powder)
• 2 Tablespoons *(15 ml)* coconut oil, melted (if not using the VitaMix with a tamper or a Blendtec with the twister jar)

instructions
1. Add the shredded coconut to the blender or food processor and blend on high.
2. If using the VitaMix with a tamper or a Blendtec with the twister jar, push the coconut down while you blend. Otherwise, stop the blender and push the coconut down with a spoon, and repeat 3 times.
3. If not using a VitaMix or a Blendtec, add the melted coconut oil in and blend on high for 10 minutes.

GARLIC SAUCE

Prep Time: 5 minutes | ***Cook Time:*** 0 minutes | ***Total Time:*** 5 minutes
Yield: approx. 1.5 cups
Nutritional Data (estimates) - per tablespoon:
Calories: 80   Fat: 9 g   Net Carbohydrates: 0 g   Protein: 0 g

ingredients
- 1 head garlic, peeled
- 1 teaspoon *(5 g)* salt
- Approx. 1/4 cup *(60 ml)* lemon juice
- Approx. 1 cup *(240 ml)* olive oil

instructions
1. Place the garlic cloves and salt into the blender. Then add in around 1/8 cup of the lemon juice and 1/2 cup of olive oil.
2. Blend well for 5-10 seconds, then slow your blender down and drizzle in more lemon juice and olive oil alternately until a creamy consistency forms.

EASY GUACAMOLE

Prep Time: 10 minutes | ***Cook Time:*** 0 minutes | ***Total Time:*** 10 minutes
Yield: 1 cup
Nutritional Data (estimates) - per tablespoon:
Calories: 40   Fat: 4 g   Net Carbohydrates: 1 g   Protein: 1 g

ingredients

- 2 ripe avocados, flesh scooped out
- 1 small tomato, diced
- 1/4 cup *(8 g)* cilantro, finely chopped
- Juice from half a lime
- Salt to taste
- 1 jalapeño, finely chopped *(optional)*
- 1/2 teaspoon *(1 g)* chili powder *(optional)*
- 1 teaspoon *(3 g)* garlic powder *(optional)*
- 1 teaspoon *(2g)* onion powder *(optional)*

instructions
1. Mash up the avocado flesh using a spoon or fork. Mix in the other ingredients.

Drinks & Broths

CHAPTER 7

EASY BONE BROTH

Prep Time: 5 minutes | **Cook Time:** 10 hours | **Total Time:** 10 hours 5 minutes
Yield: 8-16 servings
Nutritional Data (estimates) - per serving:
Calories: 80   Fat: 2 g   Net Carbohydrates: 0 g   Protein: 12 g

ingredients
- 3-4 lbs *(1.5-2 kg)* of bones *(I typically use beef bones)*
- 1 gallon *(4 l)* water *(adjust for your slow cooker size)*
- 2 Tablespoons *(30 ml)* apple cider vinegar or lemon juice

instructions
1. Add everything to the slow cooker and cook on the low setting for 10 hours.
2. Cool the broth, then strain and pour broth into a container.
3. Store the broth in the refrigerator or freezer until you're ready to use it.
4. Scoop out the congealed fat on top of the broth *(optional, but the broth is otherwise very fatty)*.
5. Heat broth when needed *(with spices, vegetables, etc)*.

After you've made the first batch of broth, you can make additional batches with the same bones. Typically, bones will last for at least 4-5 batches of broth.

COCONUT MASALA CHAI

Prep Time: 5 minutes | *Cook Time:* 5 minutes | *Total Time:* 10 minutes
Yield: 2 servings
Nutritional Data (estimates) - per serving:
Calories: 300   Fat: 30 g   Net Carbohydrates: 2 g   Protein: 3 g

ingredients
- 1 cup *(240 ml)* coconut milk
- 1 cup *(240 ml)* water
- Stevia to taste (optional)
- 1 Tablespoon *(2 g)* loose black tea leaves
- Pinch of masala tea spice blend *(recipe below)*

Masala tea spice blend:
1 Tablespoon *(7 g)* nutmeg, 1 Tablespoon *(5 g)* ginger powder, 1 Tablespoon *(6 g)* cardamom, 1 Tablespoon *(5 g)* black pepper, 1 Tablespoon *(8 g)* cinnamon, 1 teaspoon *(2 g)* cloves, 1 Tablespoon *(5 g)* dried basil *(optional)*, ground into a powder

instructions
1. Heat the coconut milk and water in a saucepan.
2. Add in the stevia, the tea, and the spice blend. Mix well.
3. Heat at a low simmer for approx. 4-5 minutes.
4. Taste the tea and add more sweetener or spices to taste.
5. Pour through a strainer *(to remove the tea leaves)* and serve immediately.

GINGER BASIL TEA

Prep Time: 5 minutes | *Cook Time:* 0 minutes | *Total Time:* 5 minutes
Yield: 2 servings
Nutritional Data (estimates) - per serving:
Calories: 0   Fat: 0 g   Net Carbohydrates: 0 g   Protein: 0 g

ingredients
- 2 cups *(480 ml)* boiling water
- 1/2 teaspoon *(1 g)* fresh ginger, grated *(or 10 very thin slices of ginger)*
- 4 fresh basil leaves

instructions
1. Add the ginger and basil to a cup or teapot and pour boiling water into the cup/teapot.
2. Brew for 5 minutes. Enjoy hot or cold.

PUMPKIN SPICE LATTE

Total Time: 5 minutes | **Yield:** 1 cup of coffee
Nutritional Data (estimates) - per serving:
Calories: 120   Fat: 13 g   Net Carbohydrates: 1 g   Protein: 1 g

ingredients

- 1 cup *(240 ml)* black coffee
- 1 Tablespoon *(15 g)* pumpkin puree
- 1/4 teaspoon *(1 g)* cinnamon
- 1/4 teaspoon *(1 g)* nutmeg
- Dash of cloves
- 1 Tablespoon *(15 ml)* ghee

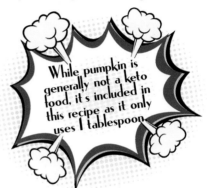

While pumpkin is generally not a keto food, it's included in this recipe as it only uses 1 tablespoon

instructions

1. Place all the ingredients into a blender and blend well for 15 seconds.

COCONUT GHEE COFFEE

Total Time: 5 minutes | **Yield:** 1 cup of coffee
Nutritional Data (estimates) - per serving:
Calories: 150   Fat: 15 g   Net Carbohydrates: 0 g   Protein: 0 g

ingredients

- 1/2 Tablespoon *(7 g)* ghee
- 1/2 Tablespoon *(7 g)* coconut oil
- 1-2 cups *(240-480 ml)* of whatever coffee you like *(or black or rooibos tea)*
- 1 Tablespoon *(15 ml)* almond milk or coconut milk

instructions

1. Put the ghee, coconut oil, almond milk *(or coconut milk),* and the coffee into a blender.
2. Blend for 5-10 seconds. The coffee turns a foamy, creamy color. Pour it into your favorite coffee cup and enjoy!
3. If you don't have a blender, then try using a milk frother.

LEMON THYME INFUSED ICED TEA

Total Time: 10 minutes + overnight infusion | *Yield:* 6-8 cups of tea
Nutritional Data (estimates) - per serving:
Calories: 0   Fat: 0 g   Net Carbohydrates: 0 g   Protein: 0 g

ingredients

- 4-6 cups *(1-1.5 l)* of black tea
- 6 sprigs of lemon thyme or other herb or spice

Grow some herbs in your garden or on your kitchen windowsill. Fresh herbs are great for adding to dishes and are also perfect for making teas.

instructions

1. Brew the black tea.
2. Remove the tea bag(s) and add 2 sprigs of lemon thyme into the hot tea.
3. Let cool and then refrigerate overnight.
4. Remove the lemon thyme and serve with ice and fresh sprigs of lemon thyme for decoration.

COCONUT ICED TEA LATTE

Total Time: 15 minutes | *Yield:* 2 cups of tea
Nutritional Data (estimates) - per cup:
Calories: 30   Fat: 3 g   Net Carbohydrates: 0 g   Protein: 0 g

ingredients

- 2 cups *(480 ml)* black tea
- 3 Tablespoons *(30 ml)* coconut milk (or to taste)
- Stevia to taste (optional)

Almond and coconut milk are great options for dairy-free milk. Just try to buy brands with as few added ingredients as possible. In particular, many brands of canned coconut milk don't have added ingredients.

instructions

1. Brew the black tea.
2. Add in the coconut milk and stevia to taste.
3. Blend for a few seconds or use a milk frother.
4. Let cool for 10 minutes, then pour into a glass with ice.

KETO DIET FOOD LIST

VEGETABLES

Try to stick to green leafy vegetables and avoid too much root vegetables to keep your daily carbohydrate intake low.

Arugula (Rocket)
Artichokes
Asparagus
Beets (not too much)
Bell Peppers
Bok Choy
Broccoli
Brussels Sprouts
Butterhead Lettuce
Cabbage
Carrots (not too much)
Cauliflower
Celery
Chard
Chicory Greens
Chives
Cucumber
Dandelion Greens
Eggplant (Aubergine)

Endives
Fennel
Garlic
Jicama
Kale
Kohlrabi
Leeks
Leafy Greens (All Kinds)
Lettuce
Mushrooms (All Kinds)
Mustard Greens
Okra
Onions
Parsley
Peppers (All Kinds)
Pumpkin (not too much)
Radicchio
Radishes
Rhubarb

Romaine Lettuce
Scallion
Shallots
Seaweed (All Sea Vegetables)
Shallots
Spaghetti Squash
Spinach
Swiss Chard
Tomatoes (not too much)
Turnip Greens
Watercress
Zucchini

FERMENTED VEGETABLES
Kimchi
Sauerkraut

FRUITS

Most fruits are off limits on a ketogenic diet. Some small amounts of berries are considered ok, but watch how much you eat!

Avocado
Blackberry
Blueberry
Cranberry
Olive

Lemon
Lime
Raspberry
Strawberry

MEATS
All cuts of the animal are good to eat, but too much protein can hamper ketosis, so watch how much you eat.

Alligator	Goose	Sheep
Bear	Kangaroo	Snake
Beef	Lamb	Turkey
Bison	Moose	Veal
Chicken	Pheasant	Wild Boar
Deer	Pork	Wild Turkey
Duck	Quail	
Elk	Rabbit	
Goat		

CURED AND PREMADE MEATS
All cuts of the animal are good to eat, but too much protein can hamper ketosis, so watch how much you eat. Also double check the ingredients to make sure there's no added sugar.

Sausages	Pepperoni	Bacon
Deli meat	Prosciutto	
Hot dogs	Salami	

ORGAN MEATS
In the United States, organ meats have fallen out of favor, but there is no other category of food that is as nutritious. Eat any of the following from pretty much any animal.

Heart	Kidney	Tongue
Liver	Bone Marrow	Tripe

GREEN BEANS + PEAS
Almost all legumes are off limits, but small amounts of green beans and peas are ok.

FATS
Fats play a huge part in the ketogenic diet (they make up the majority of your calorie intake), so make sure you're taking in plenty of healthy fats.

Avocado Oil	Palm Shortening
Ghee	Duck Fat
Coconut Oil	Butter (if you tolerate dairy)
Lard	Coconut Butter
Tallow	Cocoa Butter
Olive Oil	Walnut Oil (small amounts)
Macadamia Oil	Sesame Oil (small amounts)
Red Palm Oil	MCT Oil

FISH

Fish is highly nutritious, but buy wild-caught fish whenever possible.

Anchovies	Mahi Mahi	Tuna (including Alba-
Bass	Orange Roughy	core)
Cod	Perch	Sole
Eel	Red Snapper	Grouper
Flounder	Rockfish	Turbot
Haddock	Salmon (including	Trout
Halibut	Smoked Salmon)	Shark
Herring	Sardines	
Mackerel	Tilapia	

SHELLFISH AND OTHER SEAFOOD

Apart from organ meats, shellfish is the most nutrient-dense food you can eat. Often expensive, but worth it.

Abalone	Lobster	Scallops
Caviar	Mussels	Squid
Clams	Oysters	
Crab	Shrimp	

DRINKS

Watch out for hidden sugar in drinks!

Coconut Milk	Tea	Lemon and Lime Juice
Almond Milk	Herbal Teas	Club Soda
Cashew Milk	Water	Sparkling Mineral Water
Broth	Seltzer Water	
Coffee		

NUTS AND SEEDS

Don't go wild on these as they're easy to overeat and high in omega-6 fats. These also add to your carbohydrate intake, so watch out. Lastly, note that peanut is a legume, not a nut, and is not recommended.

Almonds	Pistachios	Walnuts
Hazelnuts	Pumpkin Seeds	Cashews
Macadamias	Psyllium Seeds	Chia Seeds
Pecans	Sesame Seeds	Various Nut Butters
Pine Nuts	Sunflower Seeds	

DAIRY

Not everyone can tolerate dairy - you should eliminate these foods for at least a month, then reintroduce them to see how they make you feel. We find raw and unpasteurized dairy to be better. Stick to full-fat dairy.

Kefir	Full-Fat Cottage Cheese	Butter (not Margarine)
Full-Fat Yogurt	Heavy Whipping Cream	Ghee
Raw Full-Fat Cheeses	Full-Fat Sour Cream	Full-Fat Cream Cheese

HERBS AND SPICES

Experiment with these herbs and spices as they'll make your food really delicious! Make sure to check the ingredients of any herb or spice blends to avoid added sugar.

Sea Salt	Cumin	Nutmeg
Black Pepper	Oregano	Cloves
White Pepper	Thyme	Allspice
Basil	Rosemary	Ginger
Italian Seasoning	Sage	Cardamom
Chili Powder	Turmeric	Paprika
Cayenne Pepper	Parsley	Dill
Curry Powder	Cilantro	
Garam Masala	Cinnamon	

OTHER

These are some foods that don't fall neatly into other categories.

Pork Rinds	Full-fat Ranch Dressing	Gelatin/Collagen
Beef Jerky	Caesar Dressing	Vanilla Extract
Pickles	Mustard	Dark Chocolate (100%)
Cod Liver Oil (Fish Oil)	Hot Sauce (check ingredients)	Stevia (small amounts if necessary)
Vinegars (check the ingredients to make sure they don't have added sugar or wheat)	Gluten Free Tamari Sauce or Coconut Aminos	Monk Fruit or Lo Han Guo Sweetener
Eggs	Fish Sauce (check ingredients)	Erythritol
Salad Dressings (check ingredients)	Cacao Nibs	Almond Flour or Almond Meal
Mayonnaise (made with good oils - see list of fats above)	Shredded Coconut	Coconut Flour
		Cacao Powder (unsweetened)

14-DAY KETO MEAL PLAN

Your first few weeks on Keto can be tough, so creating a really simple plan is the best way to stick to Keto, learn about your body, and live a healthier lifestyle long-term. The following 14-day meal plan is designed as a guide to help you create your own.

This meal plan is designed for 2 people and uses recipes from this cookbook. Please check recipe yields and make sure to halve or double the recipe accordingly.

DAY 1
Breakfast - Coconut Ghee Coffee (page 135)
Lunch - Mexican Tacos (page 61)
Dinner - Singapore-Style Noodles (page 53)

DAY 2
Breakfast - Breakfast Green Smoothie (page 13)
Lunch - Spinach Basil Chicken Meatballs (page 43) with Garlic Zucchini Saute (page 99)
Dinner - Easy Broccoli Beef Stir-Fry (page 77)

DAY 3
Breakfast - Coconut Ghee Coffee (page 135)
Lunch - Guacamole Burgers (page 69)
Dinner - Avocado Tuna Bowl (page 93)

DAY 4
Breakfast - Bacon and Fried Eggs
Lunch - Basil Chicken Saute (page 51)

Dinner - Mustard Ground Beef Saute (page 67)

DAY 5
Breakfast - Creamy Breakfast Porridge (page 17)
Lunch - Mini Burgers (page 63)
Dinner - Spaghetti Squash Bolognese (keep leftovers for dinner tomorrow) (page 66)

DAY 6
Breakfast - Breakfast Turkey Wrap (page 23)
Lunch - Big Easy Salad (page 32)
Dinner - leftover Spaghetti Squash Bolognese (page 66)

DAY 7
Breakfast - Breakfast Green Smoothie (page 13)
Lunch - Chicken Noodle Soup (page 26)
Dinner - Fish Tacos (page 88)

DAY 8

Breakfast - Almond Butter Choco Shake (page 21)
Lunch - Zucchini Beef Pho (page 59)
Dinner - Breaded Cod (page 87) with Creany Cauliflower Mash (page 102)

DAY 9

Breakfast - Breakfast Green Smoothie (page 13)
Lunch - Cucumber Ginger Shrimp (page 91)
Dinner - Beef Bacon Stew (keep leftovers for dinner tomorrow) (page 73)

DAY 10

Breakfast - Keto Toast (make Microwave Quick Bread (page 101), slice it, and toast it)
Lunch - Easy Salmon Stew (page 90)
Dinner - leftover Beef Bacon Stew (page 73)

DAY 11

Breakfast - Pumpkin Spice Latte (page 135)
Lunch - Guacamole Burgers (page 69)
Dinner - Coconut Chicken Curry (keep leftovers for dinner tomorrow) (page 48)

DAY 12

Breakfast - 2 Scrambed Eggs
Lunch - Mini Burgers (page 63)
Dinner - leftover Coconut Chicken Curry (page 48)

DAY 13

Breakfast - Breakfast Turkey Wrap (page 23)
Lunch - Chicken Noodle Soup (page 26)
Dinner - Bifteck Hache (keep leftovers for dinner tomorrow) (page 78) with Spinach Almond Saute (page 102)

DAY 14

Breakfast - 2 Fried Eggs
Lunch - Chicken Nuggets (page 47) with Creany Cauliflower Mash (page 102)
Dinner - leftover Bifteck Hache (page 78)

BATCH COOKING MEAL PLAN

No time to cook dinner every night? Then this meal plan is for you!

Pick 2-3 main dishes and 2 side dishes to cook on the weekend (make a large batch, so double or triple the recipes depending on the size of your family), then separate into individual portions and freeze. Reheat and enjoy during the week for a fast dinner.

MAIN DISHES (BEEF)
Old Fashioned Lasagna (page 57)
Mexican Tacos (page 61)
Slow Cooker Asian Pot Roast (page 70)
Beef Bacon Stew (page 73)
Slow Cooker Beef Stew (page 74)

MAIN DISHES (CHICKEN)
Spinach Basil Chicken Meatballs (page 43)
Pressure Cooker Chicken Stew (page 49)
Chicken Bacon Burgers (page 51)
Slow Cooker Jerk Chicken (page 54)
Crispy Chicken Drumsticks (page 55)

SIDE DISHES
Cauliflower White "Rice" (page 99)
Easy Bacon Brussels Sprouts (page 103)
Turmeric Cauliflower Pancakes (page 105)
Tangy Red Cabbage Coleslaw (page 106)
Cauliflower Notato Salad (page 106)
Roasted Cauliflower (page 107)